BEYOND NORMALIZATION:

Report of the UNA-USA National Policy Panel to Study U.S.-China Relations

Copies of National Policy Panel Reports are available from the
United Nations Association of the United States of America,
300 East 42nd Street, New York, New York 10017.

Cover and Layout by Christopher Rich
Design by Antupit and Others, Inc.
Printing by Dubin & Dubin 136

Library of Congress Cataloging in Publication Data

UNA-USA National Policy Panel to Study US-China
   Relations.
   Beyond normalization.

   1. United States—Relations (general) with China.
2. China—Relations (general) with the United States.
I. Title.
E183.8.C5U16   301.29'73'051   79-17784
ISBN 0-934654-21-2

ROY WERNER
Professional Staff Member
US Senate Committee on Foreign Relations

Consultants:

LYNN D. FEINTECH
Head of Political Analysis
Economics-Policy Research Department
Bank of America

BERNARD K. GORDON
Professor, Department of Political Science
University of New Hampshire

HARRY HARDING, JR.
Associate Professor, Department of
   Political Science
Stanford University

DONALD C. HELLMANN
Professor, Political Science and
   International Studies
University of Washington

JOYCE K. KALLGREN
Professor, Department of Political Science
University of California, Davis Campus;
Vice-Chairman, Center for Chinese Studies
University of California, Berkeley

CHONG-SIK LEE
Professor of Political Science
University of Pennsylvania

STEVEN I. LEVINE
Associate Professor of International Service
The American University, Washington, DC

VICTOR H. LI
Shelton Professor of International Legal
   Studies
Stanford Law School

Staff:

JOHN BRYAN STARR
Project Director

JILL A. FRIEDMAN
Associate Project Director

Administrative Staff:

JANE S. HOM

SUMMARY

Reviews developments in China's domestic and foreign politics during the eight months since the Panel was formed. Discusses reactions to normalization of US-PRC relations in the US, Taiwan, and elsewhere in Asia.

Discusses the prospects for political stability in the PRC and Taiwan. Examines the potential for future relations between Taiwan and the PRC. Considers the significance of differences of interpretation by Washington and Peking of the language of the Shanghai and normalization Communiques. Explores the legal framework for a continued informal relationship between the US and Taiwan.

Describes China's development goals and appraises the future of US economic relations with the PRC. Explores the factors affecting the continued economic viability of Taiwan and assesses the impact of normalization on it.

Details force levels of the major national actors in East Asia. Analyzes the strategic interests of China, the USSR, the Southeast Asian nations, Japan, and Korea as they relate to US strategic interests in East Asia. Assesses potential threats to the security of Taiwan.

Reviews past experience of exchanges between the US and China, describing the organizations that have been involved. Points up problems that are likely to arise as the exchange relationship develops. Reviews the significance of exchanges with Taiwan.

RECOMMENDATIONS

Based on the discussion that follows, the Panel makes the following policy recommendations:

A. POLITICAL-LEGAL ISSUES

1: The US and the PRC have a strong interest in working out peaceful, constructive relations despite what both acknowledge to be substantial differences in their economic and political systems. China's advance toward political moderation depends in part on the achievement of its economic and social development goals. The Panel recommends that the US government contribute to the achievement of these goals by continuing to act itself and to encourage private firms to act in cooperation with the Chinese in the achievement of their economic and social development aims. At the same time, both our government and the private sector should work to promote a realistic assessment by the Chinese leaders of the probable scope of that American cooperation.

2: The Panel recommends that, in its relations with the PRC, the US government continue to impress upon the Chinese leaders an accurate interpretation of the formulation the US actually agreed to in the Shanghai Communique and in the Communique issued at the time normalization was announced. The US *acknowledged* the Chinese *claim* that there is one China and that Taiwan is a part of China, but did not fully accept or "recognize" Peking's position on Taiwan. The Panel further recommends that the US government continue to emphasize its interest in a commitment to a peaceful settlement of the Taiwan issue.

3: The Panel recommends that, in its dealings with the authorities on Taiwan, the US government work to enhance the political stability of Taiwan by encouraging those authorities in their efforts to accord the Taiwanese majority a greater role in the political life of the island and to accept a natural political evolution. At the same time, the US government, and American citizens in their private dealings on Taiwan, should continue to impress the government there with the view that the extension of political freedoms and the guaranteeing of political rights are essential to the viability of the political system.

B. ECONOMIC ISSUES

4: The Panel recommends that the US government work to foster in the American business community a balanced and realistic view of the potential for future US economic interaction with China, and avoid either inflating or unnecessarily reducing this view for short-term political purposes. At the same time, it recommends that the government encourage China to rely for assistance particularly on the private business and financial communities, utilizing not only direct imports but also licensing of technology, so-called compensation agreements, joint ventures, and other techniques.

5: The Panel recommends that the Administration and Congress work together toward finding a formula by which most-favored-nation status can be granted to the PRC in order that the current imbalance in US trade with China can be at least partially corrected and that two-way trade can be expanded. However, granting MFN status should be accompanied by similar action regarding the Soviet Union in order to maintain a relatively evenhanded posture toward the two countries.

6: The Panel recommends that the Administration and Congress work together to eliminate the special requirements for the extension of government credit to non-market economies such as that of China. Moreover, the Panel supports significant additional funding for the Export-Import Bank.

7: The Panel recommends that the US government and private organizations concerned with the question explore carefully the positions of Peking and Taipei with regard to the possibility that both might sit as members in the World Bank group of institutions and in the International Monetary Fund. Assuming that the Panel's perception is correct that both sides may be prepared to explore such a possibility, the Panel recommends that the US government and relevant private organizations work closely with these international organizations to find a formula satisfactory to all members by means of which membership can be extended to the PRC without the concurrent expulsion of Taiwan.

8: In economic relations with Taiwan, the Panel recommends that the US government be cognizant of the great importance to Taiwan of US trade and investment, and that the US adopt a liberal policy toward such relations. Likewise, the import of nuclear fuel for energy purposes is vital to Taiwan, and the US should continue to make available adequate supplies under proper safeguards.

C. SECURITY AND STRATEGIC ISSUES

9: The Panel recommends that the US government pursue a policy in East Asia that seeks to enhance security interests of the countries in the region that are consonant with the US goal of the promotion of peace and security. Such a policy should involve the maintenance and strengthening of the US strategic presence in Asia, and the development of friendly relations with the people and government of the PRC.

10: The Panel recommends that US East Asian policy involve the adoption of what is here referred to as an equilibrium strategy vis-a-vis the major powers in the area, and that it resist Chinese pressure to adopt a strategy based on a united front against the Soviet Union. A policy based on an equilibrium strategy would avoid a sustained tilt toward either China or the Soviet Union, while at the same time recognizing those Soviet and Chinese defense concerns in Asia that are consonant with US global and regional security interests. The Panel recommends that the US government in its actions be sensitive to Soviet as well as Chinese perceptions of the effects of these actions on the relationship between Moscow and Peking. Finally, the Panel recommends that the US government continue to encourage Peking, Hanoi, and Moscow to resolve disputes that may arise over territorial questions by peaceful rather than violent means.

11: The Panel recommends that the US government maintain its current policy of refusing to sell weapons and technology of direct military use to the PRC. At the same time, the Panel recommends that the US government continue to permit the sale to China of advanced technology that is not of direct military use.

12: The Panel believes that the US relationship with Japan will continue to be vital to US security interests in East Asia. In the past, consultation on various issues of interest to both has sometimes been inadequate. Therefore, the Panel recommends that the US government consult more closely in the future with Japan regarding those current and future security interests in Asia and the Pacific that both nations share.

13: The Panel recommends that the US continue to discuss the problems of Korea with both Peking and Moscow, seeking to obtain their support for a realistic and peaceful evolution of relations between the two Korean states and the reduction of tension on the peninsula. The US government should also closely consult Japan on these issues.

14: The Panel supports a continued American relationship with Taiwan that will help to prevent any forceable takeover of the island by the PRC and will assist the people of Taiwan to survive as a vigorous and prosperous society capable of determining their own relationship with the mainland. The Panel believes that the US can continue to maintain a significant, independent relationship with the people of Taiwan without jeopardizing the development of a full and friendly relationship with the PRC. Accordingly, the Panel recommends that the US carry out its policy of selling carefully selected weapons for defensive purposes to Taiwan following the expiration of the Mutual Defense Treaty and until such time as a long-term and stable relationship between Taiwan and the Chinese mainland has been achieved. The US should, meanwhile, encourage flexibility on the part of both Taiwan and the PRC in the working out of such a relationship.

15: The Panel recommends that the US government continue strongly to oppose independent development of nuclear weapons by additional East Asian nations, such as Korea and Taiwan.

D. ISSUES CONCERNING SCIENTIFIC, TECHNOLOGICAL, EDUCATIONAL, AND CULTURAL RELATIONS WITH CHINA

16: The Panel believes that scientific, technological, educational, and cultural exchanges with the PRC constitute a potential source of significant mutual benefit to the US and China. Accordingly, the Panel recommends that the US government and private institutions concerned promote the development of such exchanges.

17: The Panel recommends that the roles of the US government in the development of an exchange program with the PRC include that of providing coordination and advice as requested and that of encouraging the participation of the broadest and most diverse range of individuals and groups on both sides in the program.

18: The Panel recommends that, in carrying out these roles, the US government utilize fully the proven skills and high professional expertise of the private organizations engaged in the exchange process with the PRC. The Panel further recommends that these organizations be strengthened through an increase in government funding. At the same time, independence from government control should be maintained through continued attempts to locate alternative sources of funding and development of programs which are independent of governmental sponsorship.

19: The Panel recommends the establishment by the governments of the US and the PRC of a Joint Sino-American Cultural Exchange Commission and a Joint Sino-American Science and Scholarly Exchange Commission. The majority of the American side of these commissions should be drawn from the private sector. The Panel further recommends that these commissions undertake to oversee that selection procedures for participation in exchange programs are based on peer and area review, and that selection committees are broadly based.

20: The Panel recommends that the US government and private institutions engaged in the exchange process with the PRC continue to emphasize the principles of equality and reciprocity, accepting a flexible definition of these principles.

21: The Panel recommends that the American Institute in Taiwan and private institutions maintain and expand programs of scientific, technological, educational, and cultural exchanges with Taiwan.

PREFACE

ROBERT V. ROOSA, Chairman
UNA-USA Policy Studies Committee

The National Policy Panel to Study U.S.-China Relations was formed during the late summer and early fall of 1978. Although UNA had sponsored in 1966 and 1967 two studies of the question of representation for the People's Republic of China (PRC) in the United Nations, substantial changes in the state of US-China relations over the ensuing decade made the organization of a new Policy Studies Panel seem particularly appropriate. It was clear that normalization of relations with the PRC would confront Americans with major policy issues in the not-too-distant future. Moreover, assuming that normalization occurred, even more basic questions concerning the form and substance of the new relationship would then need to be addressed, since neither academic nor government circles had given much thought to the questions, preoccupied as they were with the immediate problems surrounding normalization.

The Panel convened for its first plenary meeting in Washington on 25 October 1978. To facilitate the Panel's work, four subpanels were created, each charged with the investigation of one aspect of the broader project. One subpanel focused on Economic Aspects of the Future of U.S.-China Relations, a second on Strategic Consequences of the Evolution of U.S.-China Relations, a third on Legal Considerations in the Evolution of U.S.-China Relations, and a fourth on Scientific, Technological, Educational, and Cultural Relations with China. Each of the subpanels met for at least two sessions, at which papers commissioned for the project were read and discussed, and briefings by government and academic specialists were presented. The full Panel met for four plenary sessions involving further briefings and discussions.

Subsequent to President Carter's 15 December announcement of the normalization of relations with Peking, the Panel reassessed the scope and direction of the project. It was agreed that having such a project in being at the threshold of the new US-PRC relationship offered a unique opportunity, and that the Panel would focus its attention on the form and substance of US relations with China in the wake of normalization, as regards their economic, political-legal, strategic, and cultural and scientific aspects. The effect of normalization on US relations with Taiwan was also taken as a principal topic for consideration by the Panel. Finally, it was agreed that the US relationship with China, in order to be properly understood, had to be studied in the broader context of multipolar relations within the East Asian region.

In early March of this year, a delegation of twenty panel members and staff personnel made a two-week study tour of East Asia, stopping in Tokyo, Peking, Hong Kong, and Taipei. The delegation had more than thirty substantive discussions with government and political party leaders, with academics, with representatives of the business and professional communities, and with American diplomats stationed in the area. It was the first private organization concerned with the question of US-China relations to have visited both Peking and Taipei on the same itinerary.

Arrangements for the Asian tour were facilitated by Harvey Feldman, Richard Kilpatrick, and Lynn Pascoe of the State Department. Bian Jingzi of the staff of the Embassy of the PRC in Washington, Masuo Kawai of the staff of the Japanese Consulate in New York, and Vice Foreign Minister H. K. Yang, then representing the government of the Republic of China (ROC) in Washington, were also instrumental in making arrangements. US Ambassadors Mike Mansfield in Tokyo and Leonard Woodcock in Peking, US Consul General Thomas Shoesmith in Hong Kong, and members of their respective staffs met with the delegation and helped to facilitate arrangements during the tour. Similarly, former members of the staff of the US Embassy in Taipei, William Brown and Mark Platt, met with the delegation in Taiwan in an informal capacity while awaiting establishment of the new American Institute. Host organizations for the delegation, the Chinese People's Institute for Foreign Affairs in Peking and the ROC Foreign Ministry in Taipei, deserve particular thanks for their inexhaustible patience and hospitality. Jane Hom, of the UNA-USA staff, ably handled administrative details at the New York end, as she has throughout the study.

In addition to the information and impressions gained firsthand in Asia, the Panel benefited very much during its study from briefings and papers presented by William Barnds, Jan Berris, Ralph Clough, Lynn Feintech, Harvey Feldman, Bernard Gordon, Donald Hellmann, Kenneth Jowitt, Joyce Kallgren, Chong-sik Lee, Stephen Levine, Victor Li, Steven Olson, and Richard Solomon.

Special thanks are due to Arthur Ross, a member of UNA's

Board of Directors, for having conceived of the project and for a generous contribution that enabled us to get it under way. Funding for the project came from a number of private grants and from major contributions of the Rockefeller Foundation and the Henry Luce Foundation.

The papers commissioned by the Panel for its study are being edited by the Project Director for publication by New York University Press as part of the UNA-USA Policy Studies Book Series.

Under established policy, responsibility for UNA-USA Policy Panel Reports is taken by the members of each panel themselves. UNA-USA takes responsibility only for the choice of the subject, for selecting the panel members, for staffing and funding the project, and for publication of the report.

INTRODUCTION

A number of significant events have occurred in China and in US-China relations since the Panel began its work eight months ago. This report begins with a review of these events and of the possible trends that they may suggest.

CHINESE DOMESTIC POLITICS

In Chinese domestic politics during this period Deng Xiaoping worked to consolidate his position as first-among-equals in the Chinese leadership. Although officially he occupies a third-ranking position (behind Party Chairman and Premier Hua Guofeng and Vice Chairman and Vice Premier Ye Jianying), he nonetheless emerged as a spokesman for Chinese politics who appeared able to speak decisively without prior reference to his nominal seniors.

There is some evidence that Hua Guofeng has modified his viewpoint to coincide more closely with that of Deng. Moreover, Hua's ability to assert an independent position appears to have been weakened, as illustrated by his having been called upon to engage in self-criticism before his colleagues late last fall. Some of those who perceive factional differences between Deng and Hua argued that the flurry of "democratization" in China during recent months was encouraged by Deng expressly for the purpose of eliciting views that would undermine Hua's claim to legitimacy based on the imprimatur he received from Mao Zedong prior to the latter's death in September 1976.

This move in the direction of democratization was another particularly significant development in Chinese politics during this eight-month period. The wall poster as a vehicle for political discourse has a relatively long history in the Chinese Communist movement. It was used extensively during the Cultural Revolution to "bombard the headquarters," in Mao's phrase—to attack individuals and groups in positions of authority within the Party and state structures. The posters that were written and displayed during the fall and winter of last year, however, were more reminiscent of those produced during the Hundred Flowers Campaign of 1957 than of those from the Cultural Revolution. They were critical of Mao and his post-Great Leap Forward policies, either directly by name or indirectly using the "Gang of Four"—Mao's widow and her three radical colleagues—as surrogate targets. Deng's encouragement of the airing of opinions on wall posters and in informal publications resulted in their proliferation, particularly in Peking and the other major Chinese cities.

In addition to the more open expression of opinions, Chinese in the major cities experienced significantly increased opportunities to meet and exchange ideas with Westerners. Simultaneously, the Party began its much-publicized effort in rebuilding the legal system that had fallen into desuetude because of Mao's preference for more informal and more highly politicized practices. Discussions of this project emphasized the reinstitution of procedures to guarantee the rights of the accused. Taken together, these events suggested to some Chinese, as well as to many outside observers, that Deng and his colleagues were prepared to tolerate a situation in some respects reminiscent of that in Czechoslovakia during the "Prague Spring" of 1968.

The dissident views were not confined to criticisms of Mao, however. They also called on his successors to move more rapidly to institutionalize and guarantee the rights and freedoms contained in the Chinese constitution. As criticism began to be directed toward the socialist system and its current leaders, the leadership moved to curb its critics. Beginning in March, posters were removed from many locations in Peking; their display was restricted to specific areas; certain of the more outspoken dissidents were arrested; and the climate of burgeoning "democratization" chilled appreciably.

This outburst of public opinion was not the only source of criticism of Mao. The de facto "de-Maoization" campaign was also carried on in a cautious but persistent way at the official level by Deng and his colleagues. While the brunt of this criticism continued to focus on the surrogate targets of the Gang of Four, Mao's policies themselves increasingly came under fire in the official press. While writers stopped short of criticizing the former chairman by name, they left no doubt in their readers' minds as to the identity of their target. These criticisms appeared to be an attempt to discredit the Maoist arguments against the modernization plans of Deng and his colleagues.

The debate over Maoist principles was apparently not the only difference of opinion among the leadership. There is evidence to suggest that there were differences as well among the supporters of the new economic development policies over the scope and pace of the program. Some, apparently, initially argued that the goals were too modest and thus should be revised upward and more quickly realized. Others attempted to inject what they regarded as a note of realism into the planning process by arguing for more modest targets and a more moderate pace.

This latter debate was evidently partially resolved by the late fall of 1978 with the more moderate position prevailing. The position is elaborated in some detail in a lengthy and important article by Hu Qiaomu, President of the Chinese Academy of Social Sciences, entitled "Observe Economic Laws, Speed up the Four Modernizations" published in *People's Daily* in the late fall and in the Communique of the Third Plenum of the Eleventh Central Committee published in December. In these documents the need for realistic and fully articulated economic planning is stressed, as is reliance on the profit motive to increase the productivity of individual workers and of working units in both agriculture and industry. The need to emulate Western—particularly American—management practices is also emphasized. As discussed in greater detail below, the adoption of the more moderate approach has resulted in a reassessment in the spring of 1979 of China's development priorities, especially among different industries, as well as of its foreign exchange situation. Among other consequences this has led to a slowdown in the implementation of some of the agreements reached with foreign firms to participate in China's development process.

DEVELOPMENTS IN CHINESE FOREIGN RELATIONS

There has been no significant improvement in the state of China's relations with the Soviet Union during the past eight months. Moscow reacted to the strengthening of Chinese economic and political ties with Japan and the US by forming closer ties with Vietnam and supporting Hanoi's move against the Chinese-supported Pol Pot regime in Cambodia. The Chinese response to what they regarded as action by Hanoi prejudicial to the interests of Vietnamese citizens of Chinese ethnic origin, and to a series of incidents on the Sino-Vietnamese border, was to carry out a "punitive action" against Vietnam in February of this year. As the Chinese explained on several occasions in considerable detail to the delegation during its visit to Peking, this move had several objectives: to "teach the Vietnamese a lesson"; to undermine Hanoi's ability to support its forces in Cambodia and thereby inhibit its plan to establish an Indochinese Federation under its control; and to seek revenge for the alleged incursions of Vietnamese forces into Chinese territory. The absence of Soviet retaliation against China on Vietnam's behalf was regarded by the Chinese as an added aspect of their success and as indicative of the possibility of effective future movement to counter instances of what they regard as Soviet "expansionism" in Southeast Asia and elsewhere in the world.

The Chinese action in Vietnam, following as it did immediately Deng's visits to the US and Japan, gave rise to speculation in Moscow that Deng's plans had received at least tacit US and Japanese acquiescence. This speculation fueled Soviet concern over the possibility that a tripartite understanding might be reached between the US, Japan, and China to cooperate in opposing the expansion of Soviet influence in Asia. In fact, however, Deng had been informed by both American and Japanese officials of their opposition to China's threatened incursion into Vietnam and of their intention to deal with China and the Soviet Union in a balanced way.

These events tended to call into question one of the arguments used by the President and his advisers in their efforts to build domestic support for normalization. They had argued that full diplomatic ties between Washington and Peking would increase the degree to which American influence could be brought to bear on China's foreign policy to enhance the peace and stability of the region. Although some doubts were raised as to the forcefulness with which the US position was put to Deng during his visit, it nonetheless seemed clear that, even assuming the Chinese leaders heard and understood them, Washington's statements of disagreement had little effect on Chinese intentions to act in Vietnam.

AMERICAN RESPONSE TO NORMALIZATION

Despite this weakening of one of the Administration's arguments in support of its December actions, little effective political opposition to normalization was mounted in the American polity. Critics of the President's decision to normalize focused on what they regarded as his failure to consult adequately with Congress prior to recognizing Peking, his failure to provide US allies in Asia with sufficient advance warning, and his failure to secure a guarantee from Peking that it would not resort to the use of force in resolving the Taiwan issue. Rebutting these critics, Administration spokesmen argued that Peking's agreement to permit the US-Taiwan Mutual Defense Treaty to lapse with a year's notice in accordance with its provisions and the "agreement to disagree" over the question of future US arms sales to Taiwan were, in fact, Chinese concessions to the American position. Although movements were mounted to challenge legally the President's authority to terminate the Mutual Defense Treaty without Congressional consent and to reinstate diplomatic ties with Taiwan through Congressional action, these efforts failed to achieve any immediate, concrete results. This was partly the result of strong positive support for normalization within the business community, where, under other circumstances, conservatives would expect to find their base of support. As is discussed at greater length below, there was a certain volatility in business support for formal ties with China, as some American corporations and financial institutions tended to respond first with an unrealistic euphoria over the prospects for US-China trade, then with an equally unrealistic pessimism as the Chinese began to reassess their plan.

In January the President submitted an "omnibus bill" to Congress proposing a legal framework for the new, unofficial relationship with Taiwan. The bill set out to resolve the complex legal issues surrounding this unprecedented relationship. Its consideration in Congress was marked by much discussion over the precise terms of normalization; attempts were made to amend it both to enhance the official character of the tie with Taiwan and to raise the level of the American commitment to the island's future security. The resulting legislation, aspects of which are discussed at greater length in the sections that follow, constitutes a compromise between the Administration and Congressional positions. The Administration argued that attempts to strengthen the legislative language describing US commitments to Taiwan ran the risk of violating the understanding reached between Washington and Peking in December. The Chinese did, indeed, express their opposition to the final version of the bill in a verbal protest by Foreign Minister Huang Hua to US Ambassador Leonard Woodcock in April.

RESPONSE TO NORMALIZATION IN TAIWAN

Taiwan's reaction to the announcement of normalization was characterized more by surprise than by shock. While the authorities on Taiwan had long since accustomed themselves to the idea that US recognition of the PRC would occur at some point in the near future, several aspects of the December announcement nonetheless troubled them greatly. First, they had assumed that normalization would not take place until the spring of 1979. Moreover, President Carter believed in the need to avoid a leak of the impending announcement lest opponents of the move be given the opportunity to block it. For this reason, ROC President Chiang Ching-kuo, like other state leaders in the region, was given only a very few hours' warning of Carter's announcement. This allowed him virtually no time to prepare the people on Taiwan for the impending event. Second, ROC officials had cherished the hope that American representation on Taiwan following "de-recognition" would retain a government-to-government character, remaining at least on the level of a liaison office. Finally, the termination of the Mutual Defense Treaty and the US government's failure successfully to press Peking for a guarantee of its renunciation of the use of force against Taiwan contributed to Taipei's malaise.

The malaise was manifested most sharply during a State Department mission to Taiwan in December 1978, headed by Deputy Secretary of State Warren Christopher and charged with the task of beginning negotiations on the form of the new relationship. The Christopher delegation found itself marooned in its limousine surrounded by an actively hostile crowd. In the economic sphere there was some evidence of capital flight and of increased speculation in the Taiwanese currency on the black market. Despite these events, however, there appears to have been no "shock" to the Taiwan polity or economy of the magnitude of that which accompanied the withdrawal of Japanese recognition of Taiwan in 1972. From this January nadir in the relationship between the US and Taiwan, the situation has gradually improved.

OTHER REACTIONS TO NORMALIZATION

Reaction to the President's announcement elsewhere in Asia was generally favorable. Exceptions to this generalization were Indonesia's and Singapore's more critical positions. Japan, Korea, and the other ASEAN states were generally supportive of the US action, which many of them regarded as foreordained, and some as too long delayed. Soviet reaction was muted. Moscow made clear that establishment of diplomatic ties between Washington and Peking per se was not regarded as inimical to Soviet interests and would not preclude the successful conclusion of the SALT II negotiations. At the same time, however, Soviet leaders made clear that they would keep a close eye on the development of US relations with China and that they were unalterably opposed to American moves that could be construed as favoring China over the Soviet Union.

DEVELOPMENT OF US-CHINA TIES

Over the course of the spring, the new relationship between the US and China began to develop. During Deng's visit to Washington in January, agreements were concluded on cultural and scientific exchanges. In February, Secretary of the Treasury Michael Blumenthal visited Peking and initialed an agreement on the assets "frozen" by the two governments at the time of the Korean War. In May, Secretary of Commerce Juanita Kreps traveled to China and initialed six bilateral agreements on scientific, technological, and business cooperation. The substance and implications of these agreements are treated in some detail below.

In the sections that follow, each of the aspects of the new relationship between the US and China—political-legal, economic, strategic, and cultural and scientific—is discussed at length, and their implications for the future of US relations with Taiwan are explored. This discussion constitutes the background for the Panel's policy recommendations.

POLITICAL-LEGAL CONSIDERATIONS IN THE EVOLUTION OF US-CHINA RELATIONS

The success or failure of US relations with China is closely tied to domestic policies in both countries, as the experience of the last thirty years has shown. Following the Korean War, the Chinese leadership gave some indication of an interest in ameliorating relations with the US. The strength of anti-Communist sentiments in the American political climate of that period, however, precluded the possibility of a positive response on the part of the American government. During the 1960s, when the US government tentatively began to explore the possibility of a rapprochement with China, internal conflict in the PRC, culminating in the Great Proletarian Cultural Revolution, resulted in China's isolating itself from the world community. The Nixon Administration's exploratory moves in 1971 coincided with a period of the gradual restoration of political stability in China. These moves were prevented from coming to fruition, however, by the internal conflict in the US precipitated by the Watergate scandal and by the intense struggle over the question of the succession to Mao Zedong and Zhou Enlai in the Chinese leadership. Normalization of relations has occurred at a time when domestic politics in both political systems are in a period of relative calm and stability.

Assuming no further major political conflict in the American polity, the future of US-China relations, the maintenance of peace and stability in Asia, and the peaceful resolution of the complex "Taiwan question" are all directly dependent on the ongoing domestic political stability of the PRC and Taiwan.

The last three decades have been marked by a high degree of political stability in Taiwan, although that stability has been achieved at the cost of the full participation at all levels of the government by the "Taiwanese" majority on the island. By contrast, the same period has been one of considerable instability in the PRC, particularly at the highest levels of party and state power. Whether the political system on Taiwan will be able to prolong its history of relative stability and whether the PRC will be able to reverse its history of relative instability depend on a number of factors that are worth exploring here at greater length.

POLITICAL STABILITY IN THE PRC

The primary concerns underlying the policies of Deng Xiaoping and his colleagues since they acceded to power in 1977 have been to bring about the conditions for long-term economic growth and political stability in China. Apart from their economic substance, the long-term development plans put forward by Deng, his efforts to enter into long-term agreement with foreign governments and private firms, and his efforts at constitutional change can be seen as attempts to bind his colleagues and potential successors to the implementation and prolongation of his own views of China's future. Moreover, Deng has devoted considerable attention to the rehabilitation of those middle-level and senior cadres criticized and dismissed from their posts during the Cultural Revolution. This has enabled him both to correct what he regards as the errors of the past and to surround himself with those senior figures who share his views. More important, it puts relatively younger men and women into positions that may help them successfully to press their claim to succeed the current leaders at that point in the not-distant future when, given their advanced age, these leaders must inevitably retire from active political life.

Ideologically, Deng has attempted to lay the foundations for continued political stability by abandoning his predecessor's emphasis on class struggle as a principal tenet of political life. He argues that, because thirty years have elapsed since the seizure of state power by the Chinese Communist Party (CCP), the class distinctions that preceded that revolution have become less relevant to contemporary Chinese society than they once were. In so doing, he has abandoned Mao's view that these distinctions not only continue to influence but also are exacerbated by a bureaucratic approach to socialist development. Mao argued that differences in status, power, and wealth constitute the basis for the formation of a new bourgeois class in a socialist society, and that a series of revolutionary struggles is necessary to avoid and overcome these differences. Unlike Mao, Deng appears to believe that the need to modernize quickly outweighs the significance of the problems to which rapid modernization gives rise. Proceeding on this assumption, Deng has stated that class distinctions are no longer to be regarded as the most significant factor in China's political and economic life. Individuals formerly marked with a "bad class background" have been exonerated, and the idea that intellectuals and bureaucrats should be regarded as other than members of the working class has been renounced.

SOURCES OF SUPPORT FOR AND OPPOSITION TO DENG'S POLICIES

Assuming that progress is made toward realizing the development goals that Deng has set, many individuals and groups in Chinese society stand to gain from the attendant shift of emphasis in national priorities. Those whose careers were interrupted by the Cultural Revolution benefit from his policies of rehabilitation and reappointment. Intellectuals and intellectually gifted young people will gain from the new education system, which bases university admission primarily on competitive national examinations. They benefit as well from the abandonment of Mao's part-work, part-study system. Deng has pronounced that mental work is the equivalent of manual labor in terms of its contribution to national development and its effect on the class standing of the individual concerned.

Many workers in both industry and agriculture stand to gain from the new wage policies based on the principle that productivity can be increased through the giving or withholding of material rewards. The military in China stands to benefit from the current policies of military modernization and the revision and updating of military strategy. Finally, there are potential benefits for all Chinese that derive from the prospect of seeing their nation emerge during the twenty-first century as a major, modern power capable not only of influencing world politics but also of enhancing the quality of life in China.

On the other hand, there are those in China whose interests may not be well served by the new policies. Many middle-ranking party and government leaders owe their present position to the overturning of authority that accompanied the Cultural Revolution. In order to minimize the disruptive effects of the campaign to criticize the Gang of Four and its associates, efforts were made to restrict the number of targets at every level. Thus, while the most egregious of the "radicals" have been dismissed from their positions, presumably many more-moderate supporters of the earlier policies remain in office. Those who have been dismissed and many who remain may well see the policies of the current leaders as inimical to their interests. There are others who stand to lose under current policies. Maoist policies were based on a strong element of egalitarianism. The abandonment of what one might usefully think of as a series of "affirmative action" programs initiated under Mao's aegis is likely to affect adversely the prospects of those whom these programs were designed to benefit.

Finally, many of those who recently criticized what they regard as the oppressive policies of the last ten years are equally disaffected by Deng's qualification of his earlier position favoring democratization and his subsequent reinstitution of curbs on political freedom.

With the maintenance of political stability as their goal, two imperatives for Deng and his colleagues emerge from this potential division in Chinese society. First and most important is the attainment of the goals of the Four Modernizations. The current leaders have, by their own actions and pronouncements, made their legitimacy directly contingent upon the success of their program. Failure to make significant progress toward the realization of these goals will seriously jeopardize that legitimacy. The second imperative is the avoidance of wholesale rejection and thoroughgoing criticism of Mao and his ideas. For Deng to criticize Mao as Khrushchev criticized Stalin would be for him to risk calling into question the accomplishment of the Chinese Communist revolution as a whole, since for the CCP Mao serves, in a sense, as both the Lenin and the Stalin of that revolution. A thoroughgoing "de-Maoization" would thus weaken the legitimacy not only of the incumbents but also of the political system as a whole. Moreover, to dissociate itself completely from Mao would leave the current leadership open to the possibility that a coalition of its detractors could resurrect Mao's image as a symbolic rallying point for political opposition to his successors. As we have seen, by no means every member of such a potential coalition looks with equal favor on the Maoist approach to development and political action. Nonetheless, it would be possible for the opposition to manipulate the symbol of Mao so as to serve as an effective standard in a future political struggle in China.

POLITICAL STABILITY IN TAIWAN

The maintenance of political stability in Taiwan in the wake of the loss of US recognition would appear to pose comparable problems despite the relative lack of overt political conflict in that society in recent decades. Taiwanese society is composed of three groups. The first group, numbering fewer than 300,000, consists of the aboriginal inhabitants of the island who are ethnically distinct from the remainder of the population. Because of their small number and relative lack of development, this group is politically insignificant. Members of the second group, referred to here as the "Taiwanese," are Chinese by ethnic origin and are the descendants of those who took up residence on the island prior to 1895. This group constitutes approximately eighty-five percent of the population of roughly 17 million. The third group consists of those Chinese who came to the island following assumption of administrative control of Taiwan from Japan in 1945 and in the wake of the Chinese Communist revolution in 1949. Constituting about fifteen percent of the population, this group is referred to in this report as "mainlanders."

The legitimacy of the mainlander-dominated Kuomintang (KMT) monopolization of political power on Taiwan has rested on its claim to be the government of all of China. The government is based on a constitution adopted prior to the abandonment of the mainland following its defeat at the hands of the CCP. Its legislature, although subsequently augmented by members elected to represent the population of Taiwan, is primarily composed of aging delegates elected to represent the provinces of the mainland prior to the government's move to the island in 1949. Political power thus remains largely in the hands of the "mainlander" minority, and the freedom and rights of the Taiwanese majority are further restricted by the continued suspension of the constitution under the provision of a decree of martial law imposed in 1948. In general, this situation has proven stable largely because of the division between political and economic power that has prevailed during the last three decades. While political power rests largely in the hands of the mainlander minority, economic power is monopolized by the Taiwanese majority.

The government on Taiwan has maintained its claim to sovereignty over an undivided China and thus shares Peking's perception that "there is but one China and Taiwan is a province of China." The Taiwanese majority, on the other hand, having experienced a long history of foreign control over the island, has no interest in perpetuating the myth of a single China under ROC rule. Paradoxically, then, the group on Taiwan most adamantly opposed to the Peking regime—the mainlanders in the KMT—is the only group prepared to share with Peking an interest in future reunification; albeit with regard to the question of the auspices under which such unification might take place, the two sides are deeply and apparently unalterably divided. For the Taiwanese majority, the possibility of a closer relationship with the PRC is by no means unthinkable, though that relationship is conceived, however vaguely, as one between two sovereign, independent entities. It is the stated view of the PRC, by contrast, that the people of Taiwan favor reunification under mainland sovereignty and that it is only the domination of the KMT that is presently preventing them from realizing this interest.

Normalization of US relations with the PRC has helped precipitate a situation on Taiwan in which it is necessary for the KMT to come to grips with these problems. For a number of years the party has attempted to implement a gradual program of "Taiwanization" of

the party and government by increasing the representation of the

Taiwanese majority in both the central and local governments of the island. This process was temporarily reversed—or so it was perceived by many on Taiwan—with the decision to postpone the election for seats in the Legislative Yuan and the National Assembly scheduled to be held on the island on 23 December 1978. The UNA delegation was told by KMT officials that the election had been postponed to preclude the possibility of independent Taiwanese candidates suffering violence at the hands of those sympathetic to the plight of Taiwan and the KMT following the withdrawal of US recognition. Others have argued that the KMT took advantage of the situation to postpone an election in which many of its candidates stood to lose to non-KMT Taiwanese candidates.

During its visit to Taipei, the delegation discussed the problems of the "reconstitution" of the government on Taiwan at some length with government and party leaders, as well as with non-KMT politicians. Some evidence was found in these conversations that the KMT is giving serious thought to the need to revise state and party structure and policies to take account of the island's new political realities. An abandonment of the claim to legitimate rule over all of China, constitutional revisions, the suspension of martial law, and a revivified program of "Taiwanization" of the political system are at least under active consideration now. Electoral laws are being revised to curb recurrent violations, and a subsequent rescheduling of the December elections is planned.

American influence on the domestic policies in Taiwan has never been great, and withdrawal of recognition has done nothing to enhance that influence. Nonetheless, it is the Panel's view that such influence as remains should be brought to bear on Taipei to encourage the party and government to move in the positive directions they are currently contemplating. Prolongation of the virtual disenfranchisement of the Taiwanese majority and continued restrictions on political liberties contribute to the possibility of political instability. A Taiwan in the throes of internal political conflict would have a significant destabilizing effect in East Asia generally and on US relations with Asia particularly. The development of such a situation should be discouraged by whatever nonmilitary means are available to our government.

RELATIONS BETWEEN TAIWAN AND THE PRC

With regard to Peking's offer to negotiate to determine the future of Taiwan, little flexibility in Taiwan's position was manifested by the officials with whom the UNA delegation met in Taipei. Taiwan would agree to negotiate, the delegation was told, only if the PRC were to abandon its claim to sovereignty over the island; if it were to abandon Marxism-Leninism as the ideological foundation of its political system; if it were to transform that system so as to guarantee the political rights and freedoms of the Chinese people; and if it were to adopt a free enterprise system in place of its socialist planned economy.

The PRC position, as it was described to the delegation in Peking, contained elements of equal inflexibility beneath the surface of a series of apparently flexible overtures. As Deng Xiaoping has stated on several occasions, the Chinese have offered Taiwan the opportunity to maintain its separate political, economic, and social system if the government on Taiwan is prepared to relinquish its claim to sovereignty over the island. The authorities on Taiwan might remain in office or return to the mainland to occupy ceremonial posts within the government of the PRC. Offers have also been informally made to Taiwan to open communications links, to permit travel between the island and the mainland, and to explore the possibility of opening trade relations. On numerous occasions the Chinese have reiterated their unwillingness to renounce the use of force. To do so, it is argued, would assure that the authorities on Taiwan would never agree to negotiate. Peking has made clear, however, that it would "reluctantly" resort to force only under two sets of circumstances: first, if there were any indication of an approach by Taiwan to the Soviet Union (a move in which the authorities on Taiwan categorically deny their interest); and second, if the authorities on Taiwan continue to refuse to negotiate. The UNA delegation was unable to obtain an unambiguous answer from its Chinese interlocutors regarding the time frame involved in the second condition. In discussing this question with other individuals and groups, Deng and his colleagues have suggested limits to Peking's patience ranging from a year to a century.

Despite the apparent inflexibility of the public positions of the two sides to this dispute, there is some evidence of a different approach beneath the surface. On the PRC side, it was made clear to the delegation that so long as unification were to take place in the not-too-distant future, Peking expects to gain both economically and politically from unification with an economically viable and politically stable Taiwan. It also sees that it stands to lose from a resort to force in returning Taiwan "to the embrace of the motherland." The use of force would both alienate those nations on which the PRC is reliant in its development program and, at the same time, seriously weaken the economic fabric of Taiwan. On Taiwan's side, there is evidence of a limited willingness to interact with representatives of the PRC in ways that fall short of formal, government-to-government negotiations. Permitting individuals from Taiwan to participate alongside individuals from the PRC in academic conferences, certain sporting events, and other such circumstances is currently acceptable to both governments. Moreover, there is already under way a small amount of trade between the two, despite protestations to the contrary from Taipei. Certain raw materials are being sold by Taiwanese firms to middlemen in Southeast Asia and then resold to PRC buyers. There is also a small reverse flow of goods, at this point primarily consisting of foodstuffs. The possibilities of expanding these kinds of informal relations could be of critical importance to a peaceful resolution of the Taiwan question and are explored at greater length below.

LEGAL QUESTIONS AFFECTING US RELATIONS WITH THE PRC AND TAIWAN

For the most part, the legal framework for expanding US relations with the PRC and for maintaining informal US relations with Taiwan involves problems of economic ties and is, therefore, treated in the next section. Two questions of a legal nature, however, are of broader significance and are discussed here. The first derives from a difference in the English and Chinese language texts of two documents: the Shanghai Communique and the Communique issued by the two governments at the time that normalization of relations was announced. Whereas it is stated in the English language text of the latter document that the US government "acknowledges the Chinese position that there is but one China and Taiwan is part of China," the Chinese text uses the word *chengren* to express the English "acknowledges." Many Chinese and many American speakers of Chinese agree that a more accurate rendering of the intent of the English language text would involve substituting the Chinese term *renshi* for *chengren*, since the common translation of the latter term is more frequently "recognize" or "accept" than "acknowledge."

Beyond this linguistic difference, the UNA delegation found that Chinese officials commonly tended to distort further the American position by truncating the US statement. Omitting reference to the fact that it is a Chinese *claim* regarding the status of Taiwan that the US has acknowledged, the PRC leaders frequently gave the following version of the American point: "The United States recognizes *(chengren)* that there is one China and that Taiwan is a part of China." A further misconstruing of the American position results from the Chinese practice of referring to its agreement with the US regarding "peaceful *reunification* with Taiwan." The American position is actually one in support of "peaceful *resolution* of the Taiwan question." These phrasings have appeared frequently in the Chinese press as well as in some Chinese language periodicals in this country and Hong Kong. While the Panel does not believe that international legal complications are likely to arise due to the PRC's pressing claims based on these differences in language, it does believe that it is important for the US government to continue to make clear to Peking what it has, in fact, agreed to in these communiques. .

The second question involves the legal framework for future US relations with Taiwan. The unprecedented nature of the new relationship has required considerable legal innovation on the part of the American government. This innovation has involved the inclusion of a considerable amount of "studied ambiguity" in the resultant legislation. It is the view of the majority of the Panel members that this ambiguity, while potentially unsettling to members of a litigious society such as our own, nonetheless works to the benefit of the people of Taiwan and our relationship with them. As Victor H. Li of Stanford Law School has pointed out in a paper prepared for the Panel's use, two alternatives were available to the American government in establishing the legal basis for its relationship with Taiwan after the termination of formal diplomatic ties. The first was to treat the PRC as a "successor government" to the government of Taiwan. Choosing this alternative would have meant, among other things, that the applicability of all treaties and agreements in effect between the US and the ROC would have shifted automatically to the PRC. The second alternative—the one ultimately chosen by the Administration and endorsed by Congress—was to treat Taiwan as a "de facto entity with international personality." While the choice of this alternative requires that treaties and agreements be renegotiated with the People's Republic, it permits the maintenance of the political and legal framework for future US relations with Taiwan. Even more important, it helps to protect Taiwan against possible claims by the government of the PRC to assets held by the government of Taiwan.

The initial step in setting forth the legal framework for the new relationship came in President Carter's Executive Memorandum of 30 December 1978. There he ordered that, pending legislative action, all laws referring to unstipulated "states" or "countries" should continue to apply to "the people of Taiwan." On 26 January the President submitted to Congress an "omnibus bill," as it came to be called, providing for the establishment of the American Institute in Taiwan, the instrumentality by which the new, informal relationship was to be implemented. This Institute, incorporated in the District of Columbia, is staffed by State Department personnel who are temporarily on leave from government service for the period of their tenure with the Institute. It is headquartered in Washington and has its principal branch office in Taipei with a staff of about 50 Americans and 150 local employees. There is also a smaller branch office in Kaohsiung. The Institute's staff and activities are funded by Congress. The two offices in Taiwan carry out virtually all the functions previously performed by our Embassy and consulates. Its counterpart institute on the Taiwanese side is the Coordination Council for North American Affairs with its headquarters in Taipei, its principal branch in Washington, and lesser branches in the cities where ROC consulates existed prior to the termination of diplomatic relations.

The omnibus bill also established the legal basis for the maintenance in effect of treaties and agreements with Taiwan (except for the Mutual Defense Treaty of 1954) and for the continued applicability to Taiwan of US laws concerning international interaction that do not refer exclusively to Taiwan. Questions have been raised both in Congress and among the American public, particularly within the business and banking communities, about eliminating the bill's intentional ambiguities on the status of the government of the Republic of China under American law. It is the Panel's view that, based on the past performance of federal courts in dealing with analogous cases, the likelihood is slim that American business transactions with Taiwan would be legally jeopardized on the basis of the legislation as it was written and subsequently modified by Congress. Moreover, both American firms and their Taiwanese counterparts stand to gain from the treatment of Taiwan in that legislation as a de facto entity with international personality.

ECONOMIC ASPECTS OF THE FUTURE OF US-CHINA RELATIONS

To a large degree the Carter Administration has attempted to persuade the American public of the virtues of normalization of relations with China on economic grounds. In an effort to win support from the business community, the Administration has emphasized the positive effect on US-China trade of the formalization of ties between the two countries. While the volume of US-China trade has increased since the establishment of diplomatic relations and is likely to continue to do so, this approach has tended to foster unrealistic expectations on the part of many Americans about the rate of future growth. By contrast, indications during the last six months that the Chinese are reassessing their development program and are setting more realistic goals for themselves have given rise to an excessive pessimism among many potential traders with the PRC. It is the Panel's view that neither naive optimism nor excessive pessimism is warranted by the facts and that both are potentially counterproductive to the development of a sound economic relationship between the two countries.

CHINA'S DEVELOPMENT GOALS

In February 1978, the Chinese leadership set out a ten-year development plan to cover the period 1976 through 1985. The plan is commonly referred to as the "Four Modernizations," and is seen as the first stage in a program to develop Chinese industry, agriculture, science and technology, and defense so as to make China a fully modern socialist economy by the turn of the century. The pursuit of this development program, which is based on goals originally enunciated by former Premier Zhou Enlai, has been given first priority by Deng and his colleagues.

As it was originally enunciated, the development program envisioned the building of 120 large-scale projects, including 10 iron and steel complexes, 10 oil and gas fields, 9 nonferrous metal complexes, 8 coal mines, 30 power stations, 6 railway trunk lines, and 5 major harbors. Goals for the program included doubling steel output to an annual figure of 60 million metric tons by 1985, increasing grain production from 295 million metric tons to 400 million metric tons by 1985, and increasing electric power output at a faster rate than the increase in industrial production as a whole.

Japanese economists related to the UNA delegation their concern over the Chinese announcement in early spring 1979 that full implementation of certain contracts with Japanese firms would be delayed. During its meetings with political and economic leaders in

Peking, the delegation devoted considerable attention to the question of the significance of these announcements for the overall state of the Chinese development plan, the achievement of its goals, and the projected role of foreign economic participation in its execution.

Based on its conversations in Peking, the delegation concluded that during the late fall and early winter there had been considerable debate within the Chinese leadership regarding the scope of the goals that had been set forth and the nature and level of foreign involvement appropriate to their achievement. As has been indicated above, the result of this debate was twofold: first, the goals have been scaled down to more realistic levels; and second, the Chinese leaders have come to realize more clearly what is required to implement a complex development plan involving every sector of their economy.

The delegation was assured on several occasions that no major shifts of priorities were involved and that the modifications under way were based on questions of pace of development as opposed to fundamental questions regarding the wisdom of the program itself. Apparently, an important cause of the reassessment was the realization that China's foreign exchange earnings would be insufficient to meet the demands of the original plans for the importation of plants, equipment, and technical assistance.

Expansion and modernization of agriculture remain the top priority. Mechanization of farms, increased use of fertilizer, and improvement in seed quality all will be required. Within industry, targets for heavy industry are being reduced, with relatively more emphasis being placed on light industry. The original goal calling for a doubling of steel production to 60 million tons in 1985 is apparently now being cut to an increase of fifty percent, or 45 million tons. Energy supplies, especially electricity, remain a serious bottleneck, and expansion in this area is also accorded a high priority. The Panel was unable to obtain information on plans for the oil industry. It appears that the Chinese lack adequate knowledge of the magnitude and location of potential oil reserves. United States companies could be of particular assistance in the development of this critical resource.

In conjunction with the initial articulation of the development plan, considerable decentralization of negotiating authority took place within the Chinese system. At the same time, the authority to make decisions regarding major transactions has apparently been recentralized. While the newly acquired authority to negotiate contracts will apparently remain in the hands of provincial, county, municipal, and, in some cases, even enterprise leaders, major contracts must now be approved by the central authorities before they can be implemented. It is the lack of this approval that has caused delays in implementation or even renegotiation of certain large contracts with Japanese firms.

As has been argued above, to an important degree the legitimacy of the current leadership in the eyes of the Chinese population rests on the successful realization of the economic development goals it has set. Political stability in the PRC thus clearly rests on the economic viability of the system. It is therefore crucial to the maintenance of this stability that the leadership effectively disseminate to the Chinese population its more modest and realistic though still ambitious goals for the development program, so as to disabuse the people of their unrealizable expectations.

In this connection, the delegation became aware during the course of its conversations with Chinese leaders and American diplomats stationed in Peking and Hong Kong that the televised coverage of the visit of Deng Xiaoping to the United States in January had had an unfortunate, if perhaps unintentional, effect on Chinese viewers. For many, the coverage afforded them their first view of a fully modernized economy. It appears to have had the effect of heightening their expectations about the potential accomplishments of the Chinese development plan, while at the same time—following as it did immediately after the opening of formal ties between China and the US—heightening their expectation of what the US can contribute to the successful achievement of the goals of that plan. Just as a realistic appraisal of the future of US-China economic relations is crucial for the US business community, so too, in the Panel's view, is a realistic appraisal by the Chinese of the roles that the American government and private sector are likely to be able to play in helping to achieve China's goals. Inflated expectations with regard to American participation serve neither Chinese nor American interests.

THE AMERICAN ROLE IN CHINA'S DEVELOPMENT

In the Panel's view, economic strength and political stability in China will benefit American interests in East Asia. There are, however, constraints on the degree to which the US can contribute to China's modernization program. An initial Chinese estimate of the overall foreign and domestic investment required for the program through 1985 was $600 billion. Although the delegation was told by Vice Premier Li Xiannian that, based on a recent reassessment, this estimate was too high, nonetheless the total cost of the program will still be very great. Recent assessments of the cumulative debt capacity of the Chinese economy over the next six years project a figure of $20 to $25 billion. Two-way trade between the US and China reached the level of $1.2 billion last year. An annual increase in this figure on the order of twenty percent (in current dollars) would appear to be a reasonable projection, resulting in a two-way trade of between $4 and $5 billion by 1985. For a variety of reasons to be discussed below, projected US investment and loans to China have lagged somewhat behind the offers of credit from Japan and certain West European nations. Moreover, the scope of potential US governmental credits to China is restricted by current law. It is the Panel's view that these restrictions should be lifted in order to permit the extension of substantial government and Export-Import Bank credits to China.

In 1978, PRC imports from the US exceeded its exports to the US by a ratio of three to one. There are serious obstacles to the correction of this imbalance. To date about seventy-five percent of US exports to China have been agricultural products. To the extent that their foreign exchange and foreign credits permit, the Chinese are interested in increasing imports from the US of plants and equipment, particularly in the fields of oil exploration and extraction, iron and steel production, nonferrous metals extraction and processing, hydroelectric power generation, construction and heavy duty transport, and high-technology items such as satellites, computers, lasers, and advanced physics equipment. China's exports to the US have been concentrated in tin and tin alloys, textiles, footwear, pottery and china, specialty foods, jade and jewelry, rugs, feathers, and down. Many of these items are subject to high tariffs because China does not enjoy most-favored-nation (MFN) status. Moreover, textiles and important light industry items are areas of great protectionist pressures in the US. The Chinese have expressed their interest in exporting oil to the US, though it is clear that their ability to do so in any significant amount must await the completion of exploration and the development of additional extraction and production facilities. The amount of oil available for export will also depend upon the rate of growth of China's domestic need for petroleum products as an energy source. Nonferrous metals are another area of potential expansion of exports from China to the US, but, as in the case of oil, its expansion is subject to similar delays.

To speed up the process of expanding the trade of these commodities, the Chinese have proposed joint equity ventures and compensation trade arrangements with American and other foreign firms.

While Chinese officials in conversations with the delegation expressed some pessimism concerning the potential interest of US firms in joint equity ventures in China, they indicated considerable optimism regarding the possibilities for compensation trade arrangements. In such arrangements, a US firm would provide equipment and technical assistance for the building of a new plant in China. The plant would be constructed by the Chinese, and would employ Chinese labor for its operation. Raw materials would be imported into China by the US firm or would be of local origin. A part of the products from this plant, representing payment for equipment, technology, and other services, would be provided to US suppliers for sale in third countries or in the US. Compensation trade has been much emphasized by Chinese officials, both in public statements and in negotiating sessions since the beginning of 1979. Some small transactions of this type, involving the sale of machinery rather than whole plants, have already been concluded with American companies.

American interest in participating in arrangements of both sorts, but particularly in joint equity ventures, depends in part on the successful outcome of the project currently under way in China to develop a variety of commercial legislation. This project has been assigned to a commission of Party, state, and academic figures chaired by former Peking Mayor Peng Zhen, and is scheduled to be completed by the fall of this year. The success of China's efforts to attract foreign corporate investment and trade will be influenced by the strength and completeness of the implementation mechanisms set up. However, it is unlikely that detailed codes will be forthcoming soon, and foreign companies will probably have to work out their arrangements in contracts with Chinese trade organizations, with the new laws and regulations providing only general guidance.

A number of legal obstacles to the expansion of US economic interaction with China remained at the time of the establishment of full diplomatic relations. The first of these—the unblocking of the assets "frozen" by the two governments at the time of the Korean War—was tentatively settled in negotiations conducted during Secretary of the Treasury Michael Blumenthal's visit to Peking in the early spring, and finally signed during Secretary of Commerce Juanita Kreps' trip to China in May. Chinese assets held in the US amounted to some $80.5 million, and American assets held in China amounted to approximately $196 million. It was initially anticipated that an arrangement might be concluded with China modeled after the Litvinov Settlement with the Soviet Union in the 1930s, whereby each side took title to the assets of the other. This would have resulted in US claimants being paid at a rate of something less than forty-one cents on the dollar. It became clear, however, that the Chinese assets held in the US had been reduced since the 1970 inventory and that, as a result, payments would be significantly smaller.

During the negotiations in February, however, the Chinese agreed to pay to the US government the sum of $80.5 million over the next four years in exchange for the right to press their claim for the Chinese assets held in the US. It is the Panel's view that, under the circumstances, this settlement was a generous one on the part of the Chinese. It will result in a settlement ot US claimants of approximately forty-one cents on the dollar. Moreover, it relieves the US government of the responsibility for litigating the conflicting claims of the Chinese assets held in this country—a process which could net the Chinese, who have assumed this responsibility, considerably less than $80.5 million. Although the Chinese expressed certain reservations in signing the agreement initialed in March by Blumenthal, it was later signed without amendment, thereby opening the way for the conclusion of a trade agreement and the full-scale opening of shipping, air travel, and banking between the two countries.

The Chinese are very interested in receiving most-favored-nation status from the US, which would substantially reduce tariffs imposed on Chinese goods entering this country. While the trade agreement initialed in May grants this status, it is subject to Congressional review. A potential obstacle to the granting of Congressional approval is the Jackson-Vanik amendment to the Trade Act, which precludes the granting of nondiscriminatory treatment to those non-market economy countries that restrict the right of their citizens to emigrate. Although intended primarily as a means of pressuring the Soviet Union to lift restrictions on the emigration of Jews, the text of the amendment is applicable to China as well. There is, however, no ethnic or religious group within China comparable to Soviet Jewry. Moreover, there is evidence that the Chinese government has relaxed its emigration policies in recent months to the point that the limitation on the number of Chinese emigrants derives more from receiving countries' willingness to absorb them than it does from Chinese government restrictions. The British government's position with regard to Chinese immigration into Hong Kong is an important case in point. Nonetheless, the Carter Administration has made clear its policy that most-favored-nation status must be accorded both to the Soviet Union and China lest Moscow be given the impression that the US is "tilting" toward China.

It is the Panel's view that most-favored-nation status for China is critical to the orderly expansion of US economic interaction with the

PRC, and thus it urges speedy elimination of obstacles to its granting. Suggested ways for doing so involve expansion of the President's discretionary power to grant waivers to the amendment's provisions and Congressional suspension of its provisions for both the Soviet Union and China. Associated with these suggested approaches has been a lifting of the special requirements for government credits extended to non-market economies such as that of China. The Panel endorses this latter proposal, along with the provision of significant additional funds for the Export-Import Bank, since it will make direct government credits available to the PRC and contribute to the ability of private banks to cooperate with the Export-Import Bank in participating competitively in extending credits to China—a field presently dominated by Japan and the West European nations that do not have comparable government restrictions. With regard to the question of evenhandedness in dealing with the Soviet Union and China, it is the Panel's view that, in the economic realm as in the strategic, this principle should be applied with considerable flexibility and caution. China and the Soviet Union are at wholly different levels of economic development. A mechanically applied policy of evenhandedness in such fields as trade opportunities, transfer of technology, etc., would serve to widen the gap between the two, thus disproportionately benefiting the Soviet Union. Nevertheless, the Panel believes the two countries should be treated equally with respect to the application of such broad policies as the granting of MFN status and the ability to apply for Export-Import Bank financing.

US ECONOMIC RELATIONS WITH TAIWAN

Taiwan's economic development record over the last thirty years is impressive. Not only has the rate of growth been rapid, attaining the level of thirteen percent for the year 1978, but the achievements of the period as a whole are substantial. Among the nations of East Asia, the standard of living of the people on Taiwan is second only to that of Japan. In recent years the Taiwanese economy has demonstrated an ability to adjust to shifting markets for its goods, and has gradually begun to turn toward high-technology products and away from products involving heavy input of labor, as the cost of that labor has mounted. Moreover, the economy succeeded in weathering the "shocks" of the beginning of a dialogue between Peking and Washington, the shift in Japanese diplomatic recognition from Taiwan to the

PRC, the loss of representation in the United Nations, and the world oil crisis of the early 1970s.

The US maintains a very substantial interest in the Taiwanese economy. Two-way trade between the US and Taiwan is approaching the level of $8 billion annually—more than five times that between the US and the PRC. Some forty percent of Taiwanese exports are directed to the US market. Private banks in this country have extended nearly $3 billion in loans to Taiwan, and the Export-Import Bank has lent an additional $2 billion. Direct private US investment in Taiwan amounts to about $500 million at the present time. Thus the future economic viability of Taiwan is of direct concern to the US government and to the American business community.

It is the Panel's view that the continued economic viability of Taiwan is also perceived by the PRC as being in its own best interest. In public statements and in comments made to the delegation, Chinese leaders have indicated their concern for the maintenance of a strong economy on Taiwan with close links to the international market. The delegation was led to believe that since Chinese leaders regard Taiwan as a province of China that will some day be "reunited" with the mainland, they would prefer that reunification involve a strong, rather than a dependent and weak, economy on Taiwan.

The future economic viability of Taiwan is closely linked to the continued security of the island and to the maintenance of political stability. It is crucial to Taiwan's ability to weather the critical shock of US withdrawal of diplomatic recognition that the American government and private firms dealing with Taiwan act in a manner that bolsters, rather than undermines, the morale of the people on Taiwan. The delegation was told by the Minister of Economic Affairs in Taipei that the announcements by the Export-Import Bank that it would continue to make loans to Taiwan; by Citibank that it will continue to plan a new headquarters building and extend new credits to Taiwan; and by General Electric, General Motors, Bechtel, and Combustion Engineering that they will proceed with new joint equity ventures on the island are examples of economically and psychologically helpful actions that enhance the stability of Taiwan's economy following the termination of diplomatic relations with the US.

While believing that the prospects for the continued economic viability of Taiwan are reasonably good, the Panel is also aware of the fact that the economy, dependent as it is on foreign trade, will remain particularly vulnerable to such external factors as the price of oil, the availability of markets for its exports, and a continued inflow of investment from abroad. It is important that Americans concerned for

Taiwan's future avoid erroneously attributing fluctuations in the Taiwan economy resulting from these factors to the effects of the normalization of US relations with the PRC.

A number of legal questions arose in conjunction with the normalization of US relations with the PRC concerning the future of economic interaction between the US and Taiwan. Many of these questions were addressed in the Taiwan omnibus bill, which provided a framework for pseudo-official economic ties through the American Institute in Taiwan. Although Taiwan authorities initially pressed hard for an ongoing government-to-government relationship with the US during their discussions with the delegation in Taipei, they conceded that Congressional provisions for the American Institute in Taiwan were adequate to insure the political and legal framework for an effective, ongoing US-Taiwan economic interaction.

The omnibus bill provides that, for commercial and other purposes, Taiwan be treated as a friendly country under US law, despite the withdrawal of US recognition of the government of the ROC. This means that bank assets and other intangible assets and obligations of the ROC are unaffected by the loss of official recognition. It also means that Taiwan will retain its eligibility to benefit under such US laws as the Atomic Energy Act of 1954, the Export-Import Bank Act, the Foreign Assistance Act of 1961—including provisions affecting overseas private investment insurance—and trade laws including most-favored-nation status. Given Taiwan's increasing reliance on nuclear energy as a source of electric power on the island, the insurance of a continuation of the supply of nuclear fuel is of particular importance. Of no less significance is the continued coverage of US investment in Taiwan under the insurance provisions of the Overseas Private Investment Corporation (OPIC), since this coverage will help to alleviate any decline in the confidence of US investors with regard to new or old investments in the Taiwan economy.

WORLD BANK AND INTERNATIONAL MONETARY FUND MEMBERSHIP

During the course of its discussions in both Peking and Taipei, the UNA delegation raised the question of the possible entry of the PRC into membership in the World Bank group of institutions and the International Monetary Fund. Chinese leaders in Peking were responsive to the idea of membership in these agencies, but indicated that the contributory and reporting requirements might delay their pursuing this possibility over the near term. Most interesting was an informal comment by one government official to the effect that simultaneous membership by Peking and Taipei was not out of the question as far as Peking was concerned. These same questions were raised in Taipei, where the delegation was told that being forced to leave these agencies would have little effect on Taiwan's economy. On the other hand, Taiwan's leaders indicated their reluctance to lose their membership in these agencies because, in accordance with the provisions of the Vienna Formula, continued membership permits its representatives to attend, should they choose to do so, meetings of any of the other UN specialized agencies. In his response to the delegation's questions, a Foreign Ministry official implied that Taiwan would consider remaining in these agencies after the PRC had been seated if the PRC raised no objections.

It is the Panel's view that PRC membership in these agencies is to be encouraged, since it will enhance China's economic position and, at the same time, significantly enhance the availability of statistical information on the Chinese economy. Beyond this, the Panel believes that, if a suitable formula can be found and both sides in fact prove willing, Taiwan should remain a member of these agencies. Within these international economic forums, the two governments might conceivably meet informally to begin the long process of discussion and negotiation through which, it is hoped, their differences may at some point be peacefully resolved.

STRATEGIC CONSEQUENCES OF THE EVOLUTION OF US-CHINA RELATIONS

As one of the major national actors in the Asia-Pacific region, the US has long maintained that its principal strategic goal in this region, as in other areas of the world, is the maintenance of peace and stability. Specific policies proceeding from this broad, fundamental goal have varied significantly over the course of the three decades since the end of World War II, in which the American role constituted a capstone, in a sense, of the half-century-long process of increasing involvement by the US as a major Pacific power.

In the immediate postwar period, the US role in East Asia was one of supervising the restructuring of regional international relations through its dominant position as an occupying force in Japan, and its somewhat reluctant participation on behalf of the Kuomintang in the final stages of the Communist revolution in China. The Chinese Communist victory and the outbreak of the Korean War brought on the assumption of a new role for the US—that of containing Communism in Asia through a policy of encirclement of China, guaranteeing the defense of Taiwan, and participating, under UN auspices, in the Korean conflict. The war in Vietnam was simultaneously the zenith of the commitment of American forces to the pursuit of this role and also the cause of its attenuation. The end of that conflict led to the adoption of a new set of American policies in East Asia predicated on the principle that peace and stability are best enhanced by diplomatic interaction among all the principal national actors in the region. Normalization of relations with the PRC was undertaken in pursuit of these objectives.

US recognition of the PRC has given rise, in the Panel's view, to six major strategic issues facing American policy makers. They are: (1) the substance of the emerging US relationship with the PRC and the strength and durability of that relationship; (2) Soviet-American relations in Asia and the effect of normalization on US-Soviet relations in Asia, Europe, and other areas of the world; (3) the effect of normalization on American and Chinese relations with the constituent states of Indochina and ASEAN; (4) the effect of normalization on US relations with Japan; (5) the effect of normalization on US and Chinese relations with the two Koreas and on the relationship between the two Korean states themselves; and (6) US-Taiwan relations, including the security of Taiwan and the eventual resolution of the question of Taiwan's future relationship to the mainland of China.

Attendant to the resolution of these issues is the principle that each of the major powers in the area has certain security interests that should be accepted by the US as legitimate and consonant with the pursuit of American security interests. Security here is defined as protection of each state both from overt military aggression and from coercion under the threat or implicit threat of such aggression. Military capability is clearly crucial to the maintenance of security thus defined, but domestic political stability and economic health represent vital components as well.

FORCE LEVELS IN EAST ASIA

Because of vast differences in the level of development of the major forces in East Asia, comparisons of force levels are difficult to make and are potentially misleading. Some basic understanding of the military forces involved in the region is, nonetheless, critical to the logic of the discussion that follows. *

China's forces are by far the most numerous in the region. Chinese armed forces now number approximately 4.3 million men and women. The Chinese army numbers about 3.6 million and is garrisoned throughout the country, with heavy concentrations in those regions contiguous with the Soviet Union and in the coastal and southern provinces. Approximately eighty divisions of local and main forces are stationed in each of these two areas. The Chinese navy, numbering some 270,000 men and somewhat more than 1,000 vessels—most of them small in draft—is divided roughly equally among the North, East, and South Sea Fleets. The naval air force has some 30,000 men and 700 shore-based aircraft. The air force of 400,000 men is equipped with some 5,000 combat aircraft. Although all three services are engaged in a program of military modernization, Chinese equipment is, for the most part, outdated and insufficient in quantity. A program of nuclear weapons and missile development has been under way for a number of years in China. It is assumed that the People's Liberation Army (PLA) has a modest stockpile of nuclear weapons and medium- and intermediate-range delivery systems presently at its disposal.

Since its relations with China began to deteriorate in the mid-1960s, the Soviet Union has concentrated a substantial force on its border with China. This force is currently estimated to number approximately forty-four divisions, including three stationed in Mongolia. The Soviet Pacific Fleet includes some seventy submarines and

---

* Figures in the following sections are drawn from the International Institute for Strategic Studies (London) publication, *The Military Balance, 1978-79.* (London: IISS, 1978).

sixty-five surface ships. Soviet forces are equipped with far more sophisticated equipment than their Chinese counterparts and are, of course, augmented with a massive arsenal of nuclear weapons and delivery systems in the USSR.

Japan's military is limited, by the provisions of the American-drafted constitution adopted during the Occupation period, to a defensive force. That force currently numbers 240,000 men. More than sixty percent of this number is in the army. The Maritime Self-Defense Force, with 41,000 men, is equipped with somewhat more than 130 vessels. The air force is manned at about the same level as the navy and is equipped with 358 combat aircraft. Defense expenditure in Japan constitutes about one percent of GNP.

North Korea maintains armed forces of about a half-million men and devotes about ten percent of its GNP to defense expenditures. More than eighty-five percent of the military manpower is concentrated in ground forces, the air force having ten percent and the navy five percent of the remaining personnel. South Korean military forces number 642,000 divided as follows: army, 560,000; navy, 32,000; marines, 20,000; and air force, 30,000. Military expenditures account for somewhat more than eight percent of GNP.

Taiwan's defense expenditures also amount to approximately eight percent of GNP. Of a total armed force of 474,000 men, the army numbers 330,000, more than a quarter of whom are deployed on the islands of Quemoy and Matsu, located just off the coast of the Chinese mainland. The marines number 39,000. The air force, which numbers 70,000 men, is equipped with some 316 combat aircraft. The navy has 35,000 men and somewhat more than 100 vessels, most of them small and outdated. Their two unarmed submarines are employed exclusively for tracking exercises. Reserve forces on Taiwan number 1.16 million men; the militia includes an additional 100,000.

In numerical terms, the armed forces of Vietnam are second only to those of China. There are 615,000 men in uniform, with the vast preponderance in the ground forces. Vietnam has a very small navy, and an air force of 12,000 men and 300 combat aircraft primarily of Soviet origin. Vietnamese paramilitary forces include 70,000 frontier guards and armed security forces, and an armed militia of about 1.5 million men and women. Vietnam's defense posture was significantly bolstered by the signing of a mutual security treaty with the Soviet Union last year.

US force levels in East Asia have been reduced since the end of the Vietnam conflict. Although there are currently 30,000 US troops in Korea, an Administration proposal to reduce this level has been debated in Washington in recent months. US forces in the Pacific are also stationed at bases in Japan, the Philippines, the Pacific islands, and Hawaii. They include one infantry division, one Marine Corps division and a Marine Air Wing, and the 31,500-strong Pacific Air Forces. In addition, the navy deploys two carriers, twenty surface combatants, a support force, and a marine contingent in the western Pacific-based US Seventh Fleet. Withdrawal of US forces on Taiwan, begun at the time of the signing of the Shanghai Communique, was completed in late April 1979. The US Taiwan Defense Command moved a small skeleton staff to Hawaii, where it will operate until the termination of the 1954 Mutual Defense Treaty on 31 December 1979.

CHINA'S STRATEGIC INTERESTS

China's present strategic interests are seen by the Panel as fivefold. First, and most important, is the protection of the territorial integrity of the PRC. This involves resolution of continuing territorial disputes with the Soviet Union, India, and Vietnam. The latter dispute involves not only the land border separating China from Vietnam but also the unresolved question of sovereignty over the Paracel and Spratley island groups in the South China Sea.

A second strategic interest, closely linked to the first and often treated by the Chinese as of even greater concern, is the prevention of the spread of Soviet influence in East Asia. The Chinese seek to pursue this interest both by their own actions, such as the incursion into Vietnam in February 1979, and by encouraging alliances with the US, intermediate powers such as Japan and the West European nations, and members of the third world, directed against Moscow. In addition, China has pursued this objective by moving closer to East European nations such as Romania and Yugoslavia that have adopted a policy of limited independence from Moscow.

China's third strategic interest is to prevent the formation of a Vietnamese-controlled Indochina Federation, incorporating Cambodia and Laos, that leans distinctly toward the Soviet Union. Chinese support of the Pol Pot regime in its resistance to the Vietnamese invasion in the fall of 1978, its continued involvement in Laos in a technical capacity, and its February action against Vietnam are all directed, in toto or in part, toward this goal.

Its fourth strategic interest lies in preventing a situation in which control of the Korean peninsula falls into the hands of a power hostile to China. To realize this interest, China would prefer to see Korea reunited under the control of a socialist political system, with close, friendly relations with Peking and a common policy of opposition to the Soviet Union.

A final strategic interest (which in Chinese thinking would be included under the pursuit of territorial integrity) is reunification with Taiwan. As has been discussed above, the Chinese seek to accomplish this by peaceful means, and have agreed to permit Taiwan to keep economic, political, and social systems on the island that are separate and distinct from those in the mainland provinces. Peking insists, however, that the ROC abandon its claim to sovereignty over the island and refuses to renounce the use of force in resolving the question should the authorities on Taiwan remain recalcitrant.

Certain of these goals are consonant with US interests; others are potentially in conflict with them. The security of Chinese territorial integrity, particularly if peacefully pursued, is one such consonant goal. In the Panel's view, the US should take no position with regard to conflicting territorial claims between China and her neighbors except to encourage their peaceful resolutions.

There is little doubt that China's interest in limiting the Soviet presence in East Asia is consonant with American regional interests. There are, however, major questions with regard to how this strategic goal can best be met. As already indicated, the Chinese advocate forming a "united front" of nations opposed to the Soviet Union. Such a united front would include the US, China, and Japan as its principal participants, and would seek to involve West European and third world participants to the extent that these nations could be persuaded to see their interests as best served by such involvement.

This strategy rests upon the thesis that the Soviet Union is more dangerous than China. As such, the Chinese argue that the USSR is the only nation that can presently do major physical damage to the US in the event of a conflict, and hence represents the greatest threat to US security. Despite partial American concurrence in this thesis, the united front strategy nonetheless has several serious flaws from the American point of view. First and most important, a rigorously pursued united front strategy would render it difficult, if not impossible, to maintain a stable strategic balance and a dialogue between the US and the Soviet Union on such crucial issues as weapons control and the management of regional crises. Moscow will not passively submit to a united front in Asia arrayed against its interests, especially when coupled with the existing NATO alliance on its western flank. Furthermore, a united front strategy lacks the support not only of the major

West European nations but, more significantly, of Japan itself. While the Japanese government responded positively to American encouragement to sign the Sino-Japanese treaty of friendship in the fall of 1978 and, in turn, supported US recognition of the PRC, it has also repeatedly signaled its strong opposition to participation in an anti-Soviet alliance. Similarly, West German and French leaders have expressed their concern lest the new US policy toward China be directed against Moscow in such a fashion as to exacerbate their own relations with the Soviet Union. Although there is a minority in Washington who apparently support the idea of a united front strategy in a kind of escalated version of the "China card" strategy, the Panel supports the second of the two alternatives—that of an equilibrium strategy—for reasons to be discussed shortly in conjunction with a review of Soviet strategic interests in East Asia.

There are considerable differences of opinion in the US regarding whether American interests are better served by a united or a divided Indochina. A united Indochina under Hanoi's control can serve as a counterbalance to the potential spread of Chinese influence in the area. On the other hand, there is reason to believe that US interests may not necessarily be fully served by Vietnam's gaining control over Cambodia and Laos. Like the Chinese, exponents of this latter view argue that Hanoi intends to use an Indochinese Federation as the base for further expansion in Southeast Asia with Soviet backing. It is the Panel's view that US interests are best served when neither China nor Vietnam can pursue unrestrainedly its extraterritorial interests in the area, and when the ASEAN nations are capable of effectively maintaining their independence from undue overt or covert influence from either power.

Regarding China's capacity to realize its strategic goals, the Panel believes that the Chinese will have, at least in the short term, significant problems in effectively absorbing high-level military technology. The PRC currently lacks a sufficiently large support structure of highly educated personnel, research and development facilities, and an industrial infrastructure with a sufficient productive capacity. Additional difficulties exist owing to a shortage of capital and to the highly centralized command economy that inhibits creative research and development. Under these circumstances, the Panel questions both the feasibility and the advisability of a direct American effort to enhance Chinese military capabilities. The supply of aircraft, communications, and electronic warfare equipment by the US would tend to destabilize US-Soviet relations and have the unintended consequence of enhancing China's capacity to threaten its Southeast Asian neighbors and Taiwan if, at some point, it should choose to do so. On the other hand, it could not greatly bolster China's capacity to resist a Soviet attack. Therefore, on its own part, the US should not sell weapons to China at this time. With regard to the sale of military-related technology to China by its NATO allies, the Administration has adopted a policy of placing no obstacles in the way of those transactions. It is worth noting here that, although the Chinese have expressed considerable interest in the purchase of specific weapons systems in Europe, no contracts have yet been concluded. The sale of non-military advanced technology to the PRC by US suppliers, however, is permitted under existing US laws and regulations. Such sales are, in the Panel's view, acceptable and should not be actively discouraged.

In sum, normalization of relations with the PRC represents a major step in American efforts to relate to the government of China and its 900 million people. The US must continue its efforts to have friendly relations with this one-quarter of the world's population. Such relations can be helpful in achieving our goals of limiting tensions and enhancing peaceful political evolution in Asia. However, while recognizing that friendly relations with China are desirable, the US must also recognize that China is in no sense an ally, nor is it likely to become one in the foreseeable future.

SOVIET STRATEGIC INTERESTS IN EAST ASIA

In the Panel's view, the Soviet Union has the following five fundamental strategic goals in East Asia: (1) containment of Chinese power and influence; (2) prevention of the establishment of any anti-Soviet coalition; (3) placement of the US on the defensive and the separation of the US from its Pacific allies; (4) maintenance of implicit pressure on lines of sea and air communication in the Pacific; and (5) extension of Soviet influence throughout Asia. Only the first two goals can be regarded as consonant with US interests. The Panel supports cooperation with China to thwart Soviet achievement of the latter three goals.

The framework for such cooperation, as has been indicated above, must be one that includes US attempts to involve the Soviet Union in a constructive multilateral dialogue in East Asia. In the Panel's view, the US approach toward the establishment of such a framework should be what has been called an "equilibrium strategy." Such a strategy calls for: (1) the maintenance of a roughly balanced position between the Soviet Union and China; (2) the demonstration of

a willingness to broaden the dialogue and relations with each; (3) the
pursuit of negotiations when necessary on an item-by-item basis with
our national interests and those of our close allies kept foremost in
mind; and (4) the avoidance of any sustained tilt toward either major
Communist state. The problems inherent in implementing such a policy consistently have already been alluded to in the section dealing
with economic considerations.

It is inevitable that strategic relations with China, to an even
greater extent than economic relations, will be substantially different
from those with the Soviet Union, since the USSR is a global power
while the PRC is, at most, a regional force. An equilibrium strategy requires that the US employ a proper balance in its dealings with Peking
and Moscow, but is designed to allow some flexibility in its application
to particular situations and issues. Obviously no strategy can be pursued in pure form, and some modifications to the equilibrium strategy
will doubtless prove necessary or desirable. On balance, however, a
strategy of equilibrium will best serve US global and regional interests
in the maintenance of peace and stability.

The Panel also favors an equilibrium strategy because it takes
into account the common interest of the US and China in limiting
Soviet influence in Asia, while also recognizing that the Soviet Union
has defense concerns in East Asia that are consonant with American
and Chinese interests as the Panel perceives them. Soviet perceptions
of a threat in Asia will influence their policies not only in this region,
but also in Europe and Africa. The US should thus be careful to avoid
actions which would contribute to Soviet perceptions of a threat from
China or from a coalition of countries.

It is worth noting that a modest amelioration of Sino-Soviet
relations in the near term is by no means beyond the realm of possibility. Owing to the modifications inherent in the modernization strategy
of Deng Xiaoping and his colleagues, the major ideological differences with regard to domestic development policies—one cause of
the division between the two countries during the 1960s—have largely
disappeared. If territorial differences and conflicts with regard to third
countries abate at some point in the future, an improvement of relations between Moscow and Peking would logically follow. China
would benefit from such a situation in terms of the resources it could
recoup from the substantial concentration of troops now on the northern border. A limited detente would be consonant with US security interests in the region, since it would substantially reduce the danger of
a massive conflagration into which both sides might well attempt to
draw the US. A substantial warming of relations between Peking and

Moscow, however, would release Soviet troops and other military assets from the Chinese border. Such assets would then be available for redeployment to the Soviet western front in Europe—a situation that would clearly not be in the US interests. American policy making should be alert to and prepared for such a shift in the confrontational posture in which China and the Soviet Union presently face one another lest we be caught unprepared by such an eventuality.

THE STRATEGIC CONCERNS OF SOUTHEAST ASIA

The strategic goals of Vietnam appear to involve an attempt to impose control over a unified federation of Indochinese states, an opposition to the expansion of Chinese interests in the area, and an effort to enlist the assistance of the Soviet Union in the pursuit of the first two goals. A fourth interest, subordinated to the pursuit of the other three in recent months, is the building of links with the ASEAN nations. The strategic interests of the ASEAN nations, in turn, lie in promoting regional interaction to maximize their defensive posture against potential threats to their security from China, Vietnam, or the Soviet Union.

The initial reaction in most of Southeast Asia to normalization of US relations with China was favorable. It was treated as both an inevitable and a potentially beneficial step. Ultimately, however, normalization may come to be regarded by some in Southeast Asia as having failed to enhance the stability of the area. It now appears that a confrontation between China and the Soviet Union is more likely to arise in conjunction with problems in third countries than over border disputes. Indeed, in May, the Chinese told UN Secretary-General Kurt Waldheim that it might be necessary to "teach the Vietnamese another lesson" if efforts to negotiate their dispute continue to be unsuccessful. This poses the prospect of a prolongation of instability in the area, a prospect that can scarcely be appealing to the people of Southeast Asia, given the course of their recent history.

The Chinese view of Southeast Asia is complex. Unlike the Soviet Union, China has both geographical proximity and close cultural links to several Southeast Asian nations. The PRC, however, regards Vietnam as having become excessively ambitious, and views the Soviet-Vietnamese alliance as "part of Soviet global preparations for war." Fearing the combined efforts of what they refer to as the "lesser" and the "greater hegemonists," China clearly intends to do everything possible to forestall the formation of a Vietnamese-controlled Indochinese Federation.

Chinese efforts to carry out this intention by "teaching the Vietnamese a lesson" in February 1979 met with mixed results. Chinese leaders described to the UNA delegation at some length the lessons they derived from this action. First, and most important, was the lesson that it is necessary to act rather than remain impotent in the face of Soviet and Vietnamese expansionism. Second, the Chinese argued that their experience proved that the Soviet Union, if challenged, would not retaliate. Only if Moscow is permitted to carry out its expansionist policies in Southeast Asia and elsewhere will it continue to appear threatening. Third, the Chinese contended that their action proved the need for an alliance to act against hegemonism, since China alone was insufficiently strong to act as frequently and widely as was called for under present circumstances. Finally, we believe that the Chinese see their action in Vietnam as having demonstrated the deficiencies of equipment, coordination, and strategy in the PLA. The goals of military modernization are likely to be modified on the basis of this experience. Whether it will alter the priorities assigned to the military among the Four Modernizations remains an open question, though it seems clear that the Chinese leaders—civilian and military alike—remain convinced that a thoroughly modern industrial infrastructure is a prerequisite to the successful modernization of national defense.

The US should also learn a lesson from the recent events in Vietnam. While deploring the Chinese attempt to make it appear as though Deng Xiaoping had secured both American and Japanese approval before undertaking the invasion, the US should recognize that it can have very little influence, if any, over the relationships among Vietnam, China, and the Soviet Union. Despite this fact, the Panel believes that the US should continue to make known its opposition both to Vietnamese incursions into Cambodia and to Peking's attempt to use force in place of diplomacy in its relationship with Hanoi.

THE EFFECT OF NORMALIZATION ON US RELATIONS WITH JAPAN

Normalization is generally congenial to the Japanese for a variety of political, economic, and cultural reasons. Current Sino-Japanese relations are cordial. Tokyo is eager to help fuel the Chinese industrial revolution. Peking is not only anxious to receive Japanese assistance but also to do whatever it can to abet tension between Japan and the Soviet Union. For their part, the Japanese are interested in pursuing a policy of "proper balance" between China and the Soviet Union. As explained by a Foreign Ministry official to the UNA delegation in Tokyo, this policy is one that takes account of the special interests shared by Peking and Tokyo, and of the generally poor state of Soviet-Japanese ties. Nonetheless, it is also a policy that rejects Chinese suggestions to form a united front against Moscow.

If Japanese leaders had misgivings regarding the most recent moves in US-China relations, these misgivings were primarily occasioned by Washington's failure to consult with Tokyo prior to announcing the impending change in relations with Peking. Once again, the Japanese had reason to question the American assertion that US-Japanese relations are the keystone to American policy in East Asia.

This misunderstanding reveals a need for an ongoing redefinition of the relationship between the US and Japan, and for clarification of the meaning of existing treaty obligations in the light of the new set of relations in Northeast Asia. A new framework for consultation and cooperation between the US and Japan is clearly needed to preserve and develop this important relationship. The US should consult closely with Japan and with the ASEAN nations regarding current and future security issues pertaining to the PRC specifically and to East Asia more generally, since these nations share many of our strategic interests in the region.

KOREA AND STRATEGIC INTERESTS OF THE MAJOR POWERS

The primary strategic interest of the Democratic People's Republic of Korea (DPRK) appears to be the reunification of the two Korean states under a socialist state and a planned economy. In pursuit of this goal, North Korea has developed close ties with Peking for purposes of garnering Chinese economic and military assistance. Wary of excessive influence from its enormous northern neighbor, however, Pyongyang has attempted to balance that influence somewhat by maintaining cool but correct relations with the Soviet Union. The Republic of Korea (ROK) has not fully supported the goal of reunification, believing that even if the framework for a unified state did not require the establishment of a socialist system, South Korea would nonetheless be subject to subversion in the process of uniting with its northern rival. South Korea's strategic interests have thus involved the avoidance of attack or subversion from the North, and the building and maintenance of international ties designed to enhance ROK security, particularly those with the US, Japan, and Taiwan.

The Panel believes that the normalization of relations between the US and China may contribute to the potential for an improvement of the security situation of Korea. As we have seen, two of the most heavily armed states in Asia coexist on the Korean peninsula. The US, China, and the Soviet Union all have vital interests in these two states, given the history of the last thirty years.

In the past, the DPRK has tilted toward the PRC and away from the Soviet Union. In exchange, Peking has given full and public support to the North Korean position of opposition to opening negotiations with the ROK. The Panel believes that normalization may foster a gradual shift in the PRC position. The ROK and the PRC have begun to manifest an interest in moving toward contact with one another. Such a move on Peking's part, however, would raise the possibility of an attempted countermove by the Soviet Union, which has been interested in exploring opportunities to break the close Pyongyang-Peking links. Thus, while US relations with China may serve as a restraint, reducing the likelihood that China will support an invasion of the ROK by the DPRK, the Chinese are also bound by their fear that, were they to take a strong position in this direction, Moscow might then "play its Korean card."

The Panel believes that the US should continue to press for the opening of negotiations between the two Korean states, while at the same time engaging the PRC in discussions regarding the Korean situation. The US should seek to obtain Peking's support for a realistic and peaceful evolution of relations between the two Koreas and the reduction of tension on the peninsula. Simultaneous consultation and cooperation with Japan in this process are also essential.

THE SECURITY OF TAIWAN

Taiwan's security interests are clear-cut. Their primary concern is the maintenance of the security of the island from external attack. The goal of reconquering the Chinese mainland has long since retreated from the realm of strategy to that of political rhetoric. In the interest of furthering its primary strategic aim, Taiwan has sought to retain diplomatic ties where they still exist, and to establish and maintain informal ties with those nations that have withdrawn recognition. The maintenance of diplomatic relations with Saudi Arabia and the development of informal ties with the US, Japan, and the ASEAN states are of particular concern.

The Panel shares the perception of the majority of members of Congress and the majority of the American people that, because of our long association with the ROC, the US has a moral commitment to help prevent an unprovoked, forceable takeover of Taiwan by the PRC and to assist the people of Taiwan to survive as a vigorous and prosperous society capable of influencing over time their own relationship with the PRC.

The leadership in Peking maintains that, because "Sino-American relations can only advance on the basis of respect for the equality and sovereignty of our two nations," US support of Taiwan in general, and arms sales to Taiwan in particular, imperil relations between China and the US. Despite this assertion, it would appear unlikely that the Chinese leaders will make Taiwan a major issue in the near term, at least. If China continues to implement its current policies, it will be heavily dependent upon the advanced industrial societies, including Japan and the US, for its development program. It will also count upon the US to serve as a global countervailing force to the Soviet Union. Under these conditions, provoking a major rupture with the US and Japan over the question of Taiwan would be a highly irrational course for Peking to follow. It thus appears probable, though by no means certain, that the US can continue to develop its relations with the PRC while at the same time maintaining significant, unofficial relations with the people of Taiwan. On balance, the development of US-China relations, while in the interests of both countries, is of more vital importance to the PRC than to the US. As a result, Peking is highly likely to acquiesce tacitly in the US relationship with Taiwan as that relationship has been fashioned by Administration and Congressional action since January 1979.

Based on this assessment of the situation, the Panel believes that the US should continue to act to enhance the security of Taiwan. This security is contingent upon several factors. Principal among them, as we have seen, are domestic political stability and continued economic strength. In addition, and assuming the continued economic and political viability of the island, military strength plays a role in Taiwan's future security. The Panel believes that the probability of a direct military assault upon Taiwan by the PRC is extremely small. Not only does the PRC currently lack the capability to launch such an assault and give no appearance of attempting to acquire such a capability, but there are also many domestic and international constraints acting against its use of force. The Panel does, however, recognize that the PRC has indicated that under certain circumstances it might not be reluctant to use force. Therefore, it appears that the best security strategy for Taiwan would be to discourage military action by the PRC by making the price of such action as high as possible. By increasing its "indigestibility," Taiwan will reduce China's inclination to move with force against the island.

While the current probability of a direct amphibious attack on Taiwan is very slight, there are various military options open to the PRC now and for the foreseeable future which fall short of assault by an invasion force. The first of these options would be an air attack on Taiwan aimed at eliminating Taiwan's air defense capability. While such an attack would damage morale on the island and international confidence in the viability of Taiwan as a political and economic entity, it would also entail tremendous losses for the PRC before Taiwan's defenses were finally breached. Moreover, it would inflict serious damage to the PRC's international image and render the reunification process with Taiwan vastly more difficult.

A blockade or a threatened blockade of Taiwan by the PRC is a somewhat more plausible option. Such a tactic is currently feasible in strict military terms with present PRC naval and air forces, including submarines. Even if only partially successful, its effects on Taiwan's economy would be quickly and sharply felt. Given China's interest in reaping the benefits of reunification with an economically strong Taiwan, however, the adverse effect on the economic viability of the island that such an action would have, combined with the negative impact on Peking's relations with Washington and Tokyo, would be likely to dissuade the PRC from selecting this option.

Finally, the PRC has the option of taking some lesser military action such as attacking a single Taiwanese ship or aircraft. Such an incident might serve to undermine confidence in Taiwan's capacity to survive. At the same time, Peking might attempt to deny responsibility for the action in order to defuse a strong, adverse international reaction. While any military action against Taiwan seems highly unlikely at present, this third option would appear to be the most likely choice from Peking's perspective, should their current reluctance to consider military initiatives change.

There are a number of ways in which Taiwan can enhance its

own defense posture. It can, for example, strengthen the defenses of its airfields and secure its aircraft against damaging air attack. It can enhance its overwater air attack capability so as to be able to resist a PRC attempt to implement a blockade using surface forces or to seize Taiwanese-held islands. It can significantly increase available forces for the defense of Taiwan itself by reducing the level of its forces on Quemoy and Matsu. Finally, it can improve its capabilities for air and undersea surveillance and air anti-submarine warfare in order to "keep PRC submarines honest," that is, to prevent their operating on the surface. These measures may seem to the PRC to be provocative, but, in the judgement of the Panel, are unlikely to evoke sustained public opposition by Peking. They involve some internal reallocations within the Taiwanese military from land to sea and air forces, as well as an investment of time and energy in training and construction work. They do not, however, require an increase in the Taiwanese defense budget. So long as Taiwan remains economically prosperous, its defense should remain affordable.

The Panel believes that the US should carry out its stated policy of selling carefully selected arms for defensive purposes to Taiwan, pending the development of a long-term and stable relationship between Taiwan and the PRC. While avoiding assumption of responsibility for the future of Taiwan, the US should, on the other hand, continue to express its interest in a peaceful settlement and help the dynamics of the situation to evolve peacefully. Since Taiwan's security will ultimately depend on its political and economic stability as well as its own efforts at self-defense, the Panel believes that US arms sales will play only a limited role in that security. Arms sales will remain important only insofar as they contribute to Taiwan's indigestibility—and therefore to the unlikelihood that the PRC would resort to the use of force to resolve the question of its future relations with the island. The US should therefore make available limited amounts of technology, aircraft, and weapons for sale to Taiwan on reasonable terms.

NUCLEAR PROLIFERATION

With regard to the security of the East Asian region as a whole, the US should strongly oppose further development of nuclear weapons by the non-nuclear nations in the region. Although the US has only a limited capacity to exert influence on the nuclear weapons development policies of the Soviet Union and China, it can exert considerable leverage on the non-nuclear states, particularly Taiwan and Korea. The Panel believes that the US should bring maximum influence to bear on the non-nuclear states of the region to inhibit their development of nuclear weapons.

SCIENTIFIC, TECHNOLOGICAL, EDUCATIONAL, AND CULTURAL RELATIONS WITH CHINA

One of the most significant developments in US-China relations during the last year has been the rapid expansion of exchanges of students, scholars, and cultural and business groups between the two countries. The development and expansion of scientific, educational, and cultural exchanges, which began shortly after President Nixon's 1972 visit to Peking, will continue, in the Panel's view, to be an important dimension of Sino-American relations.

As the Chinese themselves are the first to admit, the commitment to development expressed in China's current Four Modernizations campaign requires more than the mere importation of advanced technology from the West. It also requires a cadre of highly educated personnel to facilitate the absorption of military and high-level technology. Owing in part to the disruption of education during the last decade, China currently lacks a sufficiently large cadre. Chinese leaders hope to remedy this in part through the participation of a large number of young Chinese scholars in programs of study in the US, Western Europe, and Japan. It is anticipated that a significant percentage of these scholars will study in the United States.

The Panel believes that the proposals for scientific, technological, educational, and cultural exchanges present great opportunities for both the US and China. Such programs may enhance China's ability to modernize; strengthen her ties to the world community; and lead to the development of greater mutual understanding. In order for both sides to benefit fully from opportunities presented, it is necessary at the outset to confront the problems likely to be encountered and to organize programs in such a way as to minimize difficulties and effectively serve the needs and goals of all participants.

US ORGANIZATIONS CONCERNED WITH EXCHANGES

The United States by no means lacks experience in exchange relationships with the PRC. During the years since the initial visit of the American ping-pong team to China, many exchanges have taken place, some of them formally negotiated, the rest informally arranged. The pace of this activity has increased markedly in recent months pursuant to an agreement reached by the two governments a year ago. More than fifty Chinese scholars, mostly mid-career scientists, arrived in the US in late 1978 to conduct research and receive further training. The first group of Americans to travel under the provisions of this agreement are now in China. During the last year there has also been a marked increase in the exchange of media, music, and cultural groups, the Chinese interest in which corresponds to their relaxation of ideological constraints on art and culture. Simultaneously there has been an effort to expand the number of tourist groups visiting China. Americans with some form of expertise that they are willing to share with their Chinese hosts are particularly welcome. While earlier exchange delegations from both sides had usually been restricted to brief vists of no more than a few weeks (and this remains the case for "tour" groups), more recent exchanges have been characterized by the diversification of length, topics, and style of exchange. The Chinese have expressed an interest in discussing exchanges of longer duration and in expanding bilateral ties with individual universities and scientific organizations, as well as with some public affairs groups. Formal exchanges have also proliferated. The Chinese have suggested, and the Americans have accepted, wide-ranging proposals for exchanges between governmental agencies, such as NASA and the Department of Agriculture.

This rapidly burgeoning number of exchanges has been handled by a plethora of facilitating organizations on both the Chinese and American sides. In the US, the principal organizations concerned with exchanges have been the National Committee on US-China Relations, the Committee for Scholarly Communication with the People's Republic of China, and the National Council for US-China Trade.

The National Committee on US-China Relations (NCUSCR) was established in 1966 to encourage the national consideration of China policy by American public opinion leaders, members of the business and labor communities, and individuals from academic circles. The National Committee's initial recruitment effort was directed toward the representation of a broad spectrum of views with respect to China policy. The views of the Committee and its governing Board reflected this diversity, but the Committee was unified by a commitment to develop an American dialogue on China and US-China relations.

Unfortunately, the formation of this Committee coincided with the Cultural Revolution in China, and initially little progress could be made in establishing contact. During the resurgence of foreign contacts following the end of that movement, however, the National Committee offered to assist the American Table Tennis Association in arranging a reciprocal visit of the PRC team to the US. The successful participation of the National Committee in this project led to its assuming a major role in exchanges. As a consequence, it faced a major reassessment of its priorities. In 1975 the governing Board of the NCUSCR formally endorsed a proposal that the Committee henceforth concentrate on the facilitation of exchanges with the People's Republic of China. Its educational work in the United States was turned over to the China Council of the Asia Society.

In close cooperation with the State Department, a package of exchanges has been negotiated each year since 1975. The NCUSCR has hosted or co-hosted the visits of Chinese cultural groups, sports teams, civic leaders, and other groups to the US. It has also coordinated the arrangements for return visits of American delegations in similar fields. Funding for the National Committee has varied over the years with regard to amount and sources. It has included grants from foundations, special donations for individual projects, corporate assistance, and governmental support from the International Communication Agency (ICA) and its predecessor organization, the US Information Agency.

The Committee for Scholarly Communication with the PRC (CSCPRC) was founded in 1966. The Committee grew out of proposals by a group of American scientists and China scholars for the development of some degree of communication with the scientific and academic communities in China. The initial Committee included representatives of American foundations, major universities, and the scientific community. As was the case with the National Committee, the founding of the Committee for Scholarly Communication with the PRC coincided with the Cultural Revolution in China. Between 1966 and 1969 only three meetings were held. The possibility for exchanges picked up, however, with the advent of "ping-pong diplomacy." The CSCPRC, partly through negotiations of its own and partly through negotiations at the highest governmental levels, has carried out a series of exchange programs. Until 1978, these month-long trips by American and Chinese academics constituted the level of program development desired by the Chinese. This relatively restricted program was concurred in, if not enthusiastically supported, by the CSCPRC.

The National Council for US-China Trade has taken responsibility for a somewhat different form of exchanges. Founded in 1973, it responded to the desire expressed in the Shanghai Communique "to facilitate the progressive development of trade between [the] two countries." Working closely with its PRC counterpart organization, the China Council for the Promotion of International Trade (CCPIT), since 1975 the National Council has sponsored an annually increasing number of delegations to and from China—there are thirty-five anticipated for 1979. A private, nonprofit organization, the Council nonetheless works closely with the US Departments of State, Commerce, and Agriculture. Financing is provided by membership dues assessed to the more than 400 large and small American firms which belong to the Council.

CHINESE ORGANIZATIONS CONCERNED WITH EXCHANGES

On the Chinese side, there are six major organizations that deal with exchanges. With very few exceptions, Chinese visitors to the US in the prenormalization years traveled as members of groups sponsored or arranged by one or more of the Chinese organizations responsible for overseeing and facilitating exchanges. These same Chinese organizations were responsible for receiving American delegations in China and for designating the host organization on the basis of the nature, purpose, and particular interests of the American group.

The China International Travel Service (CITS) is responsible for the administration of programs for most "self-paying guests." In addition, it frequently assumes responsibility for arrangements in China—such as transportation, hotels, and interpreters—for groups formally hosted by other organizations.

The Chinese People's Institute of Foreign Affairs (CPIFA) was established in the early days of the PRC and receives most foreign political groups and individuals not formally guests of the government (who are the responsibility of the Ministry of Foreign Affairs). Most American Congressional delegations are hosted by this organization. The CPIFA delegation, which visited the US in July 1977, was the highest-ranking delegation to visit the US prior to the visit of Vice Premier Deng Xiaoping. It was the CPIFA that acted as the host organization for the March visit to China of the UNA delegation.

The Chinese People's Association for Friendship with Foreign Countries (CPAFFC) is responsible for receiving and sending delegations on a nongovernmental level. The All-China Sports Federation (ACSF) acts as an umbrella organization charged with supervising the arrangements for the visits of the various sports teams to and from China. Normally the specific athletic organization in the US, working in cooperation with the National Committee on US-China Relations, has hosted visiting Chinese teams in the US, while the All-China Sports Federation, together with one specific organization on the PRC side, has hosted visiting American teams.

The two remaining major Chinese organizations dealing with foreign exchanges are the China Council for the Promotion of International Trade and the Science and Technology Association of the PRC. The CCPIT, as stated earlier, is the counterpart organization for the National Council for US-China Trade. It also has extensive ties with a variety of national organizations in other countries that are engaged in commerce or that seek commercial ties with China. The Science and Technology Association of the PRC has served as the counterpart organization for the Committee for Scholarly Communication with the PRC and coordinates the exchanges of the Chinese Academies of Science, Medical Science, Social Science, and Agricultural Science. It is presently affiliated with the Chinese State Scientific and Technical Commission.

It is important to note that, unlike their American counterparts which deal exclusively with exchanges with the PRC, the organizations on the Chinese side are charged with the responsibility for facilitating exchanges with every country with which the Chinese have dealings.

THE FUTURE OF EXCHANGES BETWEEN THE US AND THE PRC

As the foregoing discussion clearly indicates, there is a multitude of organizations dealing with exchanges between China and the US. The highly expert staffs of the American organizations have repeatedly demonstrated their detailed knowledge about the feasibility of particular exchanges, the location of facilities in China, and the specific arrangements necessary for a successful delegation visit. They have also developed highly effective working relationships with their Chinese counterparts. Nonetheless, difficulties have already begun to arise on the American side due to the wide diversity of programs and the large number of participants. The responsible organizations are overburdened with the rapidly expanding number of Chinese delegations arriving in the US, and are experiencing increasing difficulties with overlapping jurisdictions and lack of coordination. Although problems have arisen from time to time with Chinese efforts to politicize the exchanges, the incidence of such problems has markedly declined, especially since the purge of the Gang of Four. Unresolved questions remain, nevertheless, with regard to access to funding and to the definition of what constitutes "reciprocity" and "mutual benefit" in an exchange program between the US and the PRC.

Based on its assessment of the development and future of the exchange program between the US and China, the Panel believes that our government should continue to encourage and support exchange opportunities with China. The government's role should be to provide coordination and advice for bilateral arrangements and proposals between citizens' groups, sports federations, scientific and technological societies, and the like, when it is solicited to do so. With respect to those programs negotiated under the Cultural Agreement signed at the time of Deng Xiaoping's visit to Washington in January 1979, the US government should emphasize diversity of participation on the American side so as to provide opportunities for a broad array of individuals in the fields of culture, sports, and education to interact with their Chinese counterparts. This can be achieved not only by the pursuit of a conscious policy by the American negotiators but also by keeping in mind the other avenues for exchange that are currently developing. Implementing this principle of diversity requires the involvement of as broad a range of American groups as possible in the process of setting priorities for exchanges.

One problem likely to be faced as exchanges continue to grow will be the question of financing. The Boston Symphony Orchestra trip in March 1979, a trip undertaken at the request of the Chinese, cost close to three-quarters of a million dollars. On the other side, what have frequently been intended as casual invitations for reciprocal visits extended by various American groups traveling in China are increasingly being taken seriously and accepted by the Chinese. These American groups often find themselves in need of monetary and organizational assistance in hosting the return delegation. Providing a limited amount of funding, coordinating such efforts, and disseminating information regarding existing sources of information and assistance would be useful and positive functions for the government, particularly during the initial stages of establishing contacts through informal exchanges.

In constructing formal programs in scholarly, cultural, and educational exchanges, the government should utilize the skill and high professional expertise of the National Committee, the Committee for Scholarly Communication, and the National Council, the three major organizations that have played a central role in the prenormalization exchange process. The government should also work to strengthen these organizations. Their value rests not only in their "service capacity," although that is clearly a positive aspect of their work, but also in their range of contacts in China and in their ability to devote energy, initiative, and responsibility to program development. The fact that the CSCPRC is based in the National Academy of Sciences and maintains close ties to the American Council of Learned

Societies (ACLS) and the Social Science Research Council (SSRC) has given the CSCPRC a strong foundation for the conduct of specialized exchanges that have characterized its work.

The National Committee has also benefited from a limited amount of governmental support. The flexibility of its arrangements has been one of its primary strengths. On some occasions it has taken primary responsibility for a program; on others, it has shared responsibility with other hosts. This ability to move with some freedom within the parameters of a broadly conceived program has enabled the Committee to respond to American interest as well as to the burgeoning Chinese interest in reciprocal visits. The Panel believes that as the proportion of government funding increases in the total budget of the NCUSCR, attention must be paid to preserving a meaningful degree of autonomy for the Committee. This can best be accomplished by insuring the National Committee's active participation in the development as well in the administration of cultural and educational programs. Its continued autonomy will also depend on the ability of the NCUSCR to raise alternative funding from the public sector and to maintain some programs of nongovernmental sponsorship. The recent experience of the Boston Symphony Orchestra in China indicated that, although difficult, the results of such an effort can be enormously successful.

The Panel believes that the US and the PRC governments should establish a Joint Sino-American Cultural Exchange Commission and a Joint Sino-American Science and Scholarly Exchange Commission as vehicles for accomplishing this goal of involving a broad range of public and private organizations in the development of exchange programs. (A Joint Science and Technology Commission was authorized in the 1979 agreement between China and the US.) These commissions should be charged both with facilitating the resolution of disputes and differences between Chinese and American participants and organizations, and with serving as "umbrella" organizations performing a coordinating function in the burgeoning exchange efforts. The commissions should also undertake to provide general priority rankings for the various programs negotiated by "lead" organizations such as the ICA and the Office of the Science Adviser.

Given the plethora of existing bureaucratic units in both China and the US, it is with some reluctance that the Panel proposes the formation of these commissions. Clearly, not all exchange programs should be subsumed under these commissions. The Panel believes, for example, that the flexibility inherent in university-to-university programs is highly desirable, and should not necessarily be regulated by a national-level commission even if it were possible to do so. Nonetheless, historical experience indicates that some form of organization is necessary to deal with the important differences between the Chinese and American sides with respect to participants, areas of exchange or research, and program matters that will inevitably emerge in the course of the exchange process. The Panel believes that arrangements to review the procedures of these commissions should be designed to prevent or at least to mitigate the natural tendency of such agencies to become ingrown and overly bureaucratized. It is not the intention of this recommendation to replace the "lead" position of either the Office of the Science Adviser or that of the ICA in the field of exchanges with the PRC, but rather to provide some mechanism outside of the existing governmental framework that can develop exchanges while remaining insulated, to the maximum extent possible, from the conflicting pressures exerted by shifts in American foreign policy. The Panel believes that these commissions should draw the majority of their members from the private sector. Moreover, the presence in these commissions of a prestigious group of Americans will serve to develop domestic American support for programs when and as they become subject to the pressures of financial constraints.

The education programs negotiated with the Chinese in the fall of 1978 have been incorporated into the exchange program negotiated during the visit of Vice Premier Deng Xiaoping. The program presently involves substantial funding for scholarly exchanges. Because of the intense competition for funding and placement in the academic marketplace, there are serious limits to the availability of nongovernmental funding available from SSRC and ACLS. The federal grants have thus come to assume great importance for individuals in completing their training, writing their dissertations, seeking job placement, and career advancement. This portion of the program has thus become a fellowship program as well as an exchange program.

Until 1979 there was little need to formalize procedures for selection of scholars as scholars-escorts or to be precise about the administrative procedures used to select individual participants. Now that the financial support available to candidates is substantial, however, it is important that the programs reflect the rigorous standards of a fellowship program as well as the needs of an exchange program. Selection procedures must, therefore, emphasize high academic standing, broad-based discipline and area support, and guidelines for acceptable projects. Selection committees should be chosen to reflect the broad-based nature of faculty; procedures for selection and rotation of membership should be reasonably specific; and those appointed to selection committees should be excluded from participation in the exchange program during the tenure of their committee membership.

Moreover, the Panel believes that it is imperative to insure that selection processes and committee appointments in the various programs of exchanges with the PRC reflect the customary features of academic fellowship selection programs. These should include peer review, area review, exclusion of government-classified research programs, and implementation of methods to enlist as wide as possible a spectrum of appropriate academic participants in the selection committees.

Finally, the Panel recognizes the difficulties in designing an exchange program based on rigid application of the principles of equality and reciprocity. Because the academic and cultural interests and needs of the two societies are so disparate, it is clear that flexibility is necessary and that reciprocal exchanges with the PRC cannot be based simply on the exchange of equal numbers of students and scholars or on a field-for-field reciprocity. For the foreseeable future a lack of balance will continue to be inherent in China's desire to learn from the much higher levels of scientific and technological development in the US, while Americans will be primarily interested in social science and humanities research in China. American area specialists in the social sciences will be seeking field work opportunities in China, and we must be aware that such projects may be viewed with some suspicion by the Chinese. It will thus be necessary for the US side to continue to press for Chinese agreement to permit qualified American social scientists to pursue legitimate research projects in China. At the same time, American scholars must give attention to the problems of applying customary standards of research in providing as much protection as possible for the right to privacy of interviewees in China.

Reciprocity should thus be sought in terms of equal access by scholars on both sides to research materials and facilities, equal opportunity to send scholars in the areas in which each side has greatest interest, and equal treatment of students-scholars with freedom from governmental interference in research.

US EXCHANGES WITH TAIWAN

The Panel also supports a commitment to the maintenance and expansion of the educational, scientific, and cultural exchange programs with Taiwan, to be facilitated by the American Institute in Taiwan for the US side and the Coordination Council for North American Affairs on the Taiwan side. In the past, Taiwan has served the American scholarly community as an invaluable resource center for the study of the Chinese language, and for research in the social sciences and humanities. Its archives remain a unique resource for historical work on China and the Chinese Revolution. The limitations on exchanges with the PRC discussed above make imperative the continued use of the opportunity to study Chinese language, culture, and history on Taiwan.

The Panel further believes that interaction in the US between students and scholars from Taiwan and those from the PRC, while problematic, will in the long run prove beneficial to both groups as well as to the US. It may prove to be one more vehicle for contact between the people of Taiwan and the people of the PRC by means of which a dialogue can begin that might ultimately lead to the resolution of the political differences between the two.

UNA-USA POLICY STUDIES COMMITTEE

Chairman:

ROBERT V. ROOSA
Partner
Brown Brothers Harriman & Company
Vice Chairman, UNA-USA

Vice Chairman:

FRANKLIN A. LINDSAY
Chairman
Itek Corporation;
Board of Directors, UNA-USA

Committee Members:

ROBERT S. BENJAMIN
Co-Chairman
Orion Pictures Corporation;
Chairman, Board of Governors, UNA-USA

CHRISTINE BESHAR
Partner
Cravath, Swaine & Moore;
Board of Directors, UNA-USA

JACOB CLAYMAN
President
Industrial Union Department, AFL-CIO;
Board of Governors, UNA-USA

HARLAN CLEVELAND
Director
Program in International Affairs
Aspen Institute for Humanistic Studies;
Board of Directors, UNA-USA

JACK T. CONWAY
Senior Vice President
Government and Labor Movement Relations
United Way of America

GAYLORD FREEMAN
Honorary Chairman
The First National Bank of Chicago;
Board of Governors, UNA-USA

ERNEST E. GROSS
Curtis, Mallet-Prevost, Colt & Mosle;
National Council, UNA-USA

JOHN HAZARD
School of Law
Columbia University

ELMORE JACKSON
Consultant
Aspen Institute for Humanistic Studies;
Board of Directors, UNA-USA

JOSEPH E. JOHNSON
President Emeritus
Carnegie Endowment for International
    Peace;
National Council, UNA-USA

PHILIP M. KLUTZNICK
Klutznick Investments;
Board of Governors, UNA-USA

HARRY W. KNIGHT
Chairman and President
Hillsboro Associates, Inc.;
Treasurer, UNA-USA

PORTER McKEEVER
Associate, John D. Rockefeller, 3rd;
Board of Governors, UNA-USA

ROBERT R. NATHAN
President
Robert R. Nathan Associates, Inc.;
Board of Directors, UNA-USA

RICHARD M. PAGET
President
Cresap, McCormick and Paget, Inc.

JEAN PICKER
Vice Chairman, UNA-USA

ROBERT A. SCALAPINO
Director, Institute of East Asian Studies
University of California, Berkeley

JOSEPH M. SEGEL
Chairman, Presidential Airways;
Board of Governors, UNA-USA

JOSEPH E. SLATER
President
Aspen Institute for Humanistic Studies;
Board of Directors, UNA-USA

PHILLIPS TALBOT
President
The Asia Society

CARROLL L. WILSON
Director
Workshop on Alternative Energy
    Strategies (WAES)
Massachusetts Institute of Technology

EDITH WILSON
Director
The Action Center;
Board of Directors, UNA-USA

CHARLES W. YOST
Special Advisor
Aspen Institute for Humanistic Studies;
Honorary Co-Chairman, UNA-USA

UNA-USA Policy Studies Staff:

ARTHUR R. DAY
Vice President

EDWARD C. LUCK
Deputy Director

TOBY TRISTER GATI
Project Director
Parallel Studies Program with the Soviet
Union

PAULA R. NEWBERG
Project Director
Policy Study Panel on US Foreign Policy
    and Human Rights

RICHARD M. SEIFMAN
Executive Director
Economic Policy Council

JOHN BRYAN STARR
Project Director
National Policy Panel to Study U.S.-China
    Relations

Administrative Staff:

GERALDINE CARUANA
NAYANA M. HEIN
JANE S. HOM
MARY OLSON
JANE PASCALE
NANCY SOBIESKI

UNA-USA is a private, nonprofit organization dedicated to broadening public knowledge about the United Nations and its multifaceted activities.

UNA-USA is a sponsor of research projects on major international issues through its National Policy Panels, its Parallel Studies Program with the Soviet Union, and its Economic Policy Council. These groups, which bring together former government officials, scholars, business and labor leaders, foundation officials, and technical experts, issue reports which have helped to shape American policy on a wide range of issues, including arms control, U.S.-China relations, population, environment, international communications, and international trade.

UNA-USA is the official coordinating body for the National UN Day Program, working together with Governors' Committees and Mayors' Committees in nearly 2,000 communities. The Association also works through a network of local chapters and more than 150 affiliated national organizations, representing a total constituency of millions of Americans.

UNA-USA is the publisher of a monthly periodical, **The Inter Dependent**, and a quarterly newsletter, as well as fact sheets and educational materials on many specific UN activities.

UNA-USA is supported mainly by membership dues, by contributions from individuals, foundations, business and labor organizations, and by income from its publications, conferences, and special activities.

UNITED NATIONS ASSOCIATION OF THE UNITED STATES OF AMERICA

WILLIAM W. SCRANTON
Chairman of the Association

ROBERT S. BENJAMIN
Chairman of the Board of Governors

JAMES S. McDONNELL
Chairman Emeritus

ROBERT M. RATNER
President

China, the United Nations and United States Policy
October 1966, 64 pages. *Chairman:* Robert V. Roosa

A second report of the China Panel, updating the issues and recommendations, was issued in September 1967, 55 pages.

Stopping the Spread of Nuclear Weapons
November 1967, 48 pages. *Chairman:* Burke Marshall

Toward the Reconciliation of Europe
New Approaches for the U.S., UN and NATO
January 1969, 36 pages. *Chairman:* Theodore C. Sorensen

Controlling Conflicts in the 1970s
April 1969, 62 pages. *Chairman:* Kingman Brewster, Jr.

World Population
A Challenge to the United Nations and its System of Agencies
May 1969, 62 pages. *Chairman:* John D. Rockefeller 3rd

Beyond Vietnam: Public Opinion and Foreign Policy
February 1970, 46 pages. *Chairman:* Arthur J. Goldberg

Space Communications
Increasing UN responsiveness to the problems of mankind
May 1971, 63 pages. *Chairman:* Robert R. Nathan

The United Nations in the 1970s
A strategy for a unique era in the affairs of nations
September 1971, 88 pages. *Chairman:* Nicholas deB. Katzenbach

Southern Africa: Proposals for Americans
December 1971, 96 pages. *Chairman:* William M. Roth

Safeguarding the Atom: A Soviet-American Exchange
July 1972, 72 pages. *Chairman:* Burke Marshall

Foreign Policy Decision Making: The New Dimensions
May 1973, 108 pages. *Chairman:* Howard C. Petersen

Science and Technology in an Era of Interdependence
January 1975, 85 pages. *Chairman:* Franklin A. Lindsay

NPT: The Review Conference and Beyond
March 1975, 36 pages. *Chairman:* W. Michael Blumenthal

**Framework for an Alliance: Options for US-Japanese
      Security Relations**
August 1975, 63 pages. *Chairman:* Edmund T. Pratt, Jr.

Controlling the Conventional Arms Race
November 1976, 87 pages. *Chairman:* Thorton F. Bradshaw;
Vice Chairman: Cyrus R. Vance

**Acts of Nature, Acts of Man: The Global Response
      to Natural Disasters**
June 1977, 90 pages. *Chairman:* Orville L. Freeman

The Global Economic Challenge
Volume I: Trade, Commodities, Capital Flows
May 1978, 84 pages. *Chairman:* Robert O. Anderson

Single copies available at three dollars. Quantity prices available
on request.
United Nations Association of the United States of America
300 East 42nd Street, New York, New York 10017